A GOLDEN JUBILEE HISTORY

The Charles Redd Center for Western Studies
at Brigham Young University
1972–2022

A GOLDEN JUBILEE HISTORY

The Charles Redd Center for Western Studies
at Brigham Young University
1972–2022

JAY H. BUCKLEY

The Charles Redd Center for Western Studies at Brigham Young University: A Golden Jubilee History, 1972–2022

Copyright © 2022 by the BYU Charles Redd Center for Western Studies

Published by the BYU Charles Redd Center for Western Studies

Cover design and interior layout by Amy M. Carlin
Cover image by Charlie and Annaley Naegle Redd

Editing by Amy M. Carlin
Punctuation and capitalization in quotations may be modernized or altered for clarity.

Ordering Information:
IngramSpark at www.ingramspark.com or
Amazon-Books at www.amazon.com
Or through your local bookstore

No part of this publication may be used or reproduced in any manner whatsoever without written permission, except in the case of brief quotations embodied in critical articles, or reviews, or for teaching purposes.

Requests for reproduction or other permission should be addressed to the Charles Redd Center for Western Studies at redd_center@byu.edu

Redd Center website: reddcenter.byu.edu

Printed in the United States of America, International, by permission

ISBN: 978-0-9986960-4-1

ALL RIGHTS RESERVED

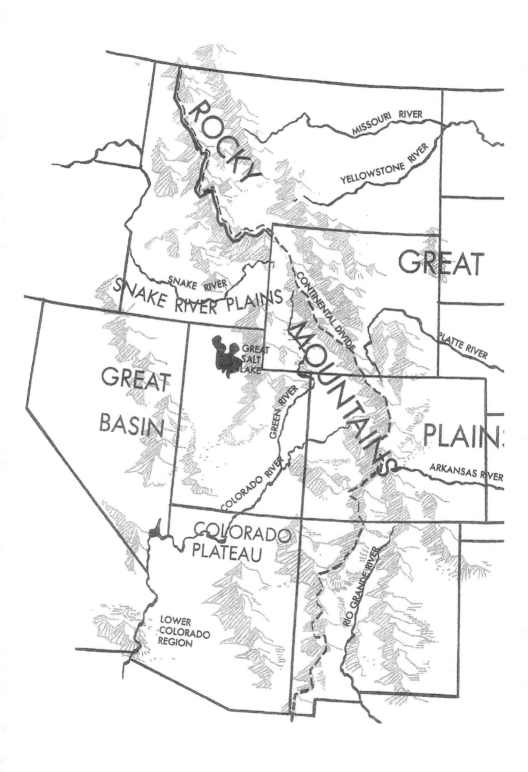

CONTENTS

ACKNOWLEDGEMENTS

Commemorating the fiftieth anniversary of the Charles Redd Center for Western Studies at Brigham Young University has been a labor of love. We are grateful for the foresight and generosity of Charlie and Annaley Redd and the continued support from their extended family. We appreciate the directors, associate directors, assistant directors, secretarial and office staff, and student employees through the years who have advanced the center's vision as one of the premier centers of the Intermountain West. We express profound gratitude to all past members of the board throughout the years for their dedication, service as judges in our annual awards competitions, and support.

Our sponsoring institution, BYU, and the College of Family, Home, and Social Sciences (FHSS) have consistently supported our efforts to provide resources for students and faculty to research and study the Intermountain West. The BYU Department of History, department Chair Brian Q. Cannon, and FHSS—especially Deans Benjamin M. Ogles and Laura M. Padilla-Walker—have been very supportive. I thank Associate Director Brenden W. Rensink and office specialist Amy Carlin for their hard work, institutional memory, and professionalism.

I am especially grateful to former Associate Director Jessie L. Embry for drafting an initial Redd Center history that served as an inspirational seed before growing and expanding exponentially into this volume. BYU undergraduate students Andra Lainhart, Camilla Richardson, Nicole (Nikki) Smith, and Emily White have been indispensable in researching, drafting, compiling, and editing content. I express my sincere gratitude to our office specialist, Amy Carlin, who completed the final editing and layout for this publication.

Finally, we honor the extended Redd, Butler, Peters, Embry, Dixon, and Taylor families for their generous financial support. In particular, we thank the Redd Foundation, Charlie and Annaley Redd, and their children—Katheryn Anne, Charles Hardison, Robert Byron, Paul David, Maraley, Beverly, Regina, and Rebecca Sue—for carrying on their parents' legacy. We dedicate this fifty-year administrative history to the Charlie and Annaley Naegle Redd family who have done so much to advance western studies throughout the Intermountain West.

Jay H. Buckley
Director, Charles Redd Center for Western Studies
Brigham Young University, Provo, Utah

BYU REDD CENTER TIMELINE

1972   Charles Redd Center for Western Studies created

1972   Lemuel H. Redd Jr. Endowment created by Charlie and Annaley Naegle Redd family

1972   Leonard J. Arrington appointed director (1972–1980)
Redd Center located in the Harold B. Lee Library

1972   Leonard J. Arrington appointed LDS Church Historian (1972–1982)

1972   First Redd Center monograph published

1973   Thomas G. Alexander hired as associate director (1973–1980)

1973   Leonard J. Arrington, Lemuel Hardison Redd Jr. Professor in Western American History, Endowed Chair (1973–1987)

1973   John Bluth hired as oral history program director (1973–1979)

1979   Jessie L. Embry hired as oral history program director (1979–2014)

1980   Thomas G. Alexander appointed director (1980–1992)

Ron W. Walker and Kenneth L. Cannon II both served terms as assistant or acting directors

1986   John Topham and Susan Redd Butler Endowment proposed by son Karl and Mollie Butler

1987   James B. Allen appointed Lemuel Hardison Redd Jr. Professor in Western American History, Endowed Chair (1987–1992)

1992   Thomas G. Alexander appointed Lemuel Hardison Redd Jr. Professor in Western American History, Endowed Chair (1992–2004)

1992   William A. (Bert) Wilson appointed director (1992–1996)

1992   Lemuel H. Redd Jr. Endowment augmented by Charles Redd Foundation

1994   Jessie L. Embry appointed assistant/associate director (1994–2014)

       Bertis L. and Anna E. C. Embry Endowment created during Jessie's employment

1995   John Topham and Susan Redd Butler Endowment created by a donation from daugher Hazel Butler and William Howard Peters

1995   Leonard J. Arrington publishes *Charlie Redd: Utah's Audacious Stockman*

1996   Edward A. Geary appointed director (1996–2002)

2001   Jessie L. Embry served as acting director (2001–2002)

2002   Brian Q. Cannon appointed director (2002–2018)

2003   Mollie and Karl Butler Young Scholar Award in Western Studies begun

2006   Ignacio M. García appointed Lemuel Hardison Redd Jr. Professor in Western American History, Endowed Chair (2006–present)

2010   Clarence Dixon Taylor Endowment established by nephew John Arthur Taylor

2013   Redd Center offices move from 366 KMBL to 954 KMBL

2015   Brenden W. Rensink hired as assistant director (2015–present)

2016   *Intermountain Histories* digital history project launched

2018   Jay H. Buckley appointed director (2018–present)

2018   *Writing Westward* podcasts initiated

2019   Brenden W. Rensink promoted to associate director (2019–present)

2020   *BYU Slavery Project* created to study the legacies of slavery pertaining to campus history

2020   Ignacio M. García Scholarship created for Indigenous and students of color in collaboration with the BYU Department of History

2021   Native American Rights Seminar launched

2022   Fifty-year commemoration of the Charles Redd Center for Western Studies

REDD CENTER MISSION STATEMENT

The mission of the Charles Redd Center for Western Studies is to promote the study of the Intermountain West by sponsoring research, publication, teaching, and public programs in a variety of academic disciplines including history, geography, sociology, anthropology, politics, economics, literature, art, folklore, range science, forestry, and popular culture.

CHAPTER 1. REDD CENTER ORIGINS: THE ARRINGTON/ALEXANDER YEARS, 1972-1980

In 1972, three factors provided the perfect formula for the establishment of the Charles Redd Center for Western Studies: (1) an increased focus of the study of the American West throughout the United States, (2) donors who believed in the preservation of the pioneer ideals, and (3) Brigham Young University's willingness to create a center with support. In 2022, the center celebrates its fiftieth anniversary by reflecting upon its founding and its evolution over the first half century.

Charlie and Annaley Naegle Redd

Charles "Charlie" Redd grew up in San Juan County, Utah, the son of Hole-in-the-Rock pioneers Lemuel Hardison Redd Jr. and Eliza Westover Redd. Charlie was the manager of the La Sal Livestock Company and spent most of his life raising cattle and sheep, always working to improve the ranch, the livestock, and the range. In addition to ranching, Charlie served in the Utah State Legislature and on the boards of trustees of Utah State University, Utah Power and Light, and Amalgamated Sugar Company. BYU English professor and friend Karl E. Young called Charlie a renaissance man because of his wide range of interests, including politics, religion, literature, science, and art. He and his wife, Annaley Naegle Redd, also traveled widely to Europe, South America, Australia, and the Far East.

Charlie and Annaley valued education. That conviction brought the Redds to Provo where their children could attend school, specifically Brigham Young High School. They built a home in Provo's close-knit Tree Streets neighborhood, where many BYU faculty members also lived. The Redds became especially close friends with BYU physics professor John Gardner and his wife, Olga. Gardner was instrumental in suggesting the Redds endow a chair and a center focused on the American West. As Charlie explained, "I would like somehow to get into the hearts and souls of young people the lessons of history, particularly those of Western America. The American pioneer has

A portrait of Charlie Redd that hangs in the 2022 Charles Redd Center
Credit: J. Roman Andrus (1907–1993), "Portrait of Charles Redd," 1972, oil on canvas, 38 1/8
x 30 inches. Brigham Young University Museum of Art, 1972.

much to teach us, with his insistence on individual freedom of action, his spirit of adventurousness and his willingness to accept challenge. He reminds us how precious is the heritage of individual freedom." He continued "Perhaps more important to youth today is how acceptance of challenge and risk-taking strengthens character and contributes to individual growth. Only through the acceptance of great challenges and the struggle with adversity is man's soul enlarged and extended. Learning of the successful settlement of this country, we may gain courage to face squarely the challenges and problems of present-day frontiers."[1]

Creation of Western Studies Centers

Charlie's belief mirrored Frederick Jackson Turner's 1893 frontier thesis that the availability of open land in the West helped shape American democracy. Turner's theory received scholarly scrutiny and reinterpretation over the years, but in the 1960s and 1970s, individuals and institutions reengaged in regional studies. According to historiographer Peter Novick, starting in the 1960s, "historians prided themselves on the extent to which their studies had been 'broadened' and 'enriched'—moving away from a focus on a very limited range of activities . . . to encompassing everything that everybody had done everywhere."[2] Western American historians followed this larger trend when they created the Western History Association in 1961. At about the same time, universities created western study centers, following a pattern of other regional, ethnic, and women's study centers created during this era.

Brigham Young University Faculty

A relatively new BYU history professor, Thomas G. Alexander, was especially interested in highlighting the Intermountain West. Looking back, he explained that the University of Utah had a "head start" in creating a center, but he felt BYU could also highlight the western region, especially since the university had at least twenty-two scholars across the campus in the late 1960s and early 1970s who specialized in the American West. For example, the history department hired seven western history scholars between 1954 and 1970. With this strong focus, Alexander and his colleagues Richard L. Bushman, James B. Allen, and Ted J. Warner requested BYU form a western studies center. Allen recalled that although Bushman was not a western historian, he was interested in the future of BYU and was influential no matter where he went.

In September 1967, Bushman presented an ambitious plan for a new center for Western American History and Culture to the BYU administration. After describing BYU's strengths in studying the West, he outlined possible programs: (1) Purchase of Frederick Remington paintings and art collections; (2) Purchase of microfilm copies of newspapers with plans to index; (3) Purchase of manuscript collections; (4) Publication of a Guide to the Study of Western History similar to the *Harvard Guide to American History*; (5) Publication of a western American atlas; and (6) Sponsorship of lectures and monograph series. Later, undated proposals scaled down these plans, but they all explained a western studies center would "benefit the university, faculty, and student body" especially if it worked in harmony with the university's Institute of Mormon Studies.[3]

Leonard J. Arrington

Leonard J. Arrington played an important role in the creation of the new center. An economics professor at Utah State University, Arrington was respected as a western and Latter-day Saint economic historian. The Redds may have already known of Arrington due to Charlie's position on the USU board of trustees. To help persuade the Redds to donate to BYU, John Gardner suggested that if BYU established a western studies center, Arrington might move from USU to BYU to lead it. Bushman recalled, "Charlie had great respect for Leonard, and John made the most of it. Charlie respected the kind of history Leonard had written and wanted more of it." After the appointment was made, Redd commented, "I am delighted with the choice of Dr. Arrington. He is an outstanding scholar who has made an important contribution to economic thought and history of the West." He trusted that Arrington's appointment would "attract interaction and attention."[4]

BYU began discussing a center for western research with the Redds in 1968 and finalized the arrangements in the early 1970s. Unfortunately, Charlie suffered a stroke during that period, leaving Annaley and their children to work out the arrangements. The Redds agreed to make an initial donation of half a million dollars to BYU to establish a chair of western history named after Charlie's father, Lemuel Hardison Redd Jr. In return, BYU agreed to create a western studies center named after Charlie Redd. BYU President Dallin H. Oaks explained the creation of the Charles Redd Center for Western Studies and the Lemuel Hardison Redd Jr. Professor of Western American History shared a common objective: "extending man's knowledge of the American West."[5]

At the same time BYU was creating the Redd Center, The Church of Jesus Christ of Latter-day Saints experienced an increased interest in academic history. Arrington and others asked the Church to appoint a professional historian, and Church leaders set their sights on Arrington. In March 1971, Martin Hickman, dean of the College of Social Science, wrote to Arrington that he hoped Arrington would consider coming to BYU soon. Hickman added that he knew Arrington desired an appointment as Church Historian, but he felt the Church and BYU might create a joint position where Arrington would direct the center, hold the endowed chair, potentially teach a class every semester, and work with PhD students. Hickman suggested either Thomas G. Alexander or James B. Allen help with the Redd Center's administrative responsibilities. In May 1971, BYU President Ernest L. Wilkinson sent Arrington a contract for $25,000 annually. In the cover letter, Wilkinson wrote that having the center would emphasize the importance of western history at BYU and he hoped it would be "the best in the nation."[6]

On November 23, 1971, Arrington began keeping a diary. In his first entry, he wrote: "It would appear that an announcement will be made shortly that I have accepted an appointment as Charles [should have read Lemuel] H. Redd Professor of History at BYU beginning January 1, 1972." He noted, "The appointment at BYU also includes serving as director of the Western History Center [Charles Redd Center]. This center will enjoy a budget, which will make possible research and publication in Western American History, lecturer fees, research fellowships, travel, and the purchase of rare books and manuscripts. According to present plans, the center will be located in the BYU library."[7]

Arrington noted his responsibilities at USU would make it necessary for him to "phase in" to the BYU position and planned to move to Provo in the fall of 1972. He asked Hickman to help pay for his moving expenses, and he started making plans to move to Provo. That move did not take place, however, because after some discussion, BYU President Dallin H. Oaks and Church leaders such as Elders Neal A. Maxwell and N. Eldon Tanner discussed the value of a joint appointment for Arrington as the Redd chair at BYU and as Church Historian. The university would pay half of his salary and the Church would pay the other half. President Oaks called Arrington on January 13, 1972, to deliver the news.[8]

Arrington wrote a personal essay about the event. "At the time of my call to be Church Historian, President Tanner informed me that he had talked with President Dallin Oaks of Brigham Young University, and that, if I agreed, I was to serve also as the Lemuel Hardison Redd Professor of Western History and the inaugural director of the Charles Redd Center for Western Studies at the university." Both of these positions, he noted "were made possible by a generous grant from Charles Redd, who made funds available for research and publication in Western American history, lecturers' fees, research fellowships, travel, and purchase of rare books and manuscripts." Arrington was to "divide my time between BYU and the Historical Department of the Church, with Tom Alexander assisting as associate director of the Redd Center." Arrington asked James B. Allen of BYU and Davis Bitton of the University of Utah to serve as the two Assistant Church Historians.[9]

Arrington determined that his first priority would be as Church Historian at the Church

James B. Allen (left), Leonard J. Arrington (center), and Davis Bitton (right)

Historian's Office for The Church of Jesus Christ of Latter-day Saints, ultimately culminating in his move to Salt Lake City instead of Provo.[10] While he planned to spend time in Provo teaching classes and coordinating the center's operation, he still needed someone to conduct the center's day-to-day activities. With Arrington's recommendation and approbation, BYU appointed Thomas G. Alexander to fill the role of associate director of the Redd Center. Alexander had completed his bachelor's and master's degrees at Utah State University, where he was Arrington's research assistant and assisted him on several publications. Alexander had joined the BYU history faculty in 1964 and received his PhD from UCLA the following year.[11] In a December 15, 1976, dairy entry Arrington elaborated on how fond he was of Alexander: "I did more of these [co-authored publications] with Tom Alexander than with any other person, and he and I worked well together; and you will note that I asked him to be my associate director of the Redd Center when it was organized at BYU."[12]

According to the press release announcing Arrington as the Lemuel Hardison Redd Chair and the creation of the "Western History Center" [Charles Redd Center for Western Studies], President Oaks envisioned an interdisciplinary center that covered "all areas of Western Americana—history, economics, geography, sociology, religion, art, music and folklore." Working with funding from the university and with the cooperation of the BYU departments, Oaks saw "immediate benefits" in teaching, expanding the library, and sponsoring research, publications, and seminars. Arrington and Alexander agreed the "basic purpose [was] the promotion of scholarly research on various aspects of American Western development ... on the part of faculty and students in a wide range of disciplines."[13] The 1973 Redd Center annual report added, "This is a research and educational center ... [where] an advisory council recommends policy which is then determined by the Dean of the College of Social Science and the Academic Vice President and implemented by the director and associate director."[14]

Even before the public announcement, Arrington and Alexander selected an advisory board with faculty from BYU, professors from other universities in Utah, and members of the Redd family. The board met just before the reception, which announced the Redd Center and honored Charlie Redd. Members included BYU professors James B. Allen, history; Wesley Burnside, art; Eugene Campbell, history; Chad Flake, Special Collections; Keith Melville, political science; John Sorensen, anthropology; and Larry Wimmer, economics. Other members were Everett Cooley, library, University of Utah; Charles S. Peterson, history, Utah State University; and Hardy Redd, the oldest son of Charlie and Annaley Redd.

First, the board discussed the Redd Center's focus and mission statement. According to Alexander, "We wanted to be different from other western studies centers. We decided to focus on the Mountain West from the outset. We used the census definition of Utah, the states surrounding Utah, and Montana." Arrington, Alexander, and the board decided the center would support western studies, not just western history. Some records list the major disciplines as history, art, literature, political science, geography, and archaeology. Another early document contains an ambitious list of topics for research and library acquisition that included Latter-day Saints, Utah, Spanish borderlands, art and artists of the West, western literature and folklore, the Great Plains, western historians, and the economic, political, social, intellectual, and cultural history of the Intermountain West.

Alexander explained in a letter to BYU administrator Robert K. Thomas that the center would work with the library, adding his hope that the center become an important "research center for Western Americana in the United States." In finalizing the mission statement, the directors and boards trimmed some of the original goals and added others. These revisions included a distinguished professorship, research and study grants, seminars, colloquia, and unique research projects coordinated by the center. The board agreed that while the center should appropriately focus on western studies, it should also include Latter-day Saint history and Mormon studies.

The Arrington/Alexander Years, 1972–1980

One early logistical concern was office space. Bushman's plan called for a reading room in the library's Special Collections, then housed in the Pioneer Room on the fourth floor. The ambitious plan was that the Redd Center would cover the fourth floor with an art gallery and offices for staff and visiting professors. While the offices were never that large, Alexander recalled that the university and library agreed to house the center in the library near Special Collections.

The center's first offices were located wherever the library had extra space. This temporary arrangement comprised of two offices on the west side of the fourth floor. Arrington had one office that stored the center's library and files, while Alexander and the part time secretary shared the other office. In 1974, the center moved to a specially designed space closer to the Pioneer Room. The new offices included a reception area and four offices for the director, assistant director, oral history program director, and research assistants. The library administrators originally offered the center a room for visiting scholars, but they ultimately assigned the space to another department.

Arrington, Alexander, and the board started working on various projects even though not all Redd funds were immediately available. An attempt to purchase some Remington paintings proved unsuccessful, and Arrington, Alexander, and the board decided that purchasing manuscript collections was too expensive. Instead, they chose to sponsor lectures and seminars, publish monographs, invite visiting scholars to teach classes and introduce center programs, hire research assistants, and provide research support grants to faculty and students.

The first visiting faculty member at the center was Gary L. Shumway—a professor from California State University, Fullerton; a native of Blanding, Utah; and a leader in student-trained oral history programs in the United States. The Redd Center hired Shumway to teach an oral history class at BYU during the summer of 1973. The year before, he started an oral history program at the Church History Department. Oral history was a way to document the new social history movement in the 1960s and 1970s. The Redd Center paid two-thirds of Shumway's salary while the history department paid the rest.

Shumway limited the class to ten students and allowed faculty to observe and learn the techniques. After an introduction to oral history, most of the students conducted interviews in Monticello and American Fork, Utah. To help provide funds for equipment, projects, and other expenses for students, Shumway contracted with these cities and the Utah State Historical Society. In addition, the center paid Charles S. Peterson and BYU graduate student Gregory Maynard to interview the family and acquaintances of Charlie Redd. Students were also free to develop their own projects. All these interviews became the basis for the Redd Center oral history program.

Alexander asked John F. Bluth, a PhD student in history, to be the teaching assistant for Shumway's class. Bluth enrolled in the class and helped produce the class handbook, find tapes and tape recorders, and develop and carry out interview plans. The oral histories conducted during this class initiated the Redd Center's oral history program. The center hired Bluth to complete processing interviews and start new projects.[15] Although the center did not have money to hire a full-time staff member, they made it work by hiring research assistants like Kris Rigby, who typed up oral history interviews. Arrington's Mormon History Trust Fund, College of Social Sciences Dean Martin Hickman, and the Utah State Historical Society provided financial support. The center applied for grants from the National Endowment for the Humanities for a project on Utah labor. Although they did not receive the grant, the college agreed to provide some money.

On October 28, 1977, Arrington recorded in a journal entry that "one of the finest things the Redd Center is doing now is conducting an oral history program. This is under the general charge of John Bluth."[16] A few years later, Bluth became the cataloguer in the library's Special Collections in 1979, so Jessie L. Embry, another member of Shumway's oral history class, was hired as director of the oral history program. After returning from a mission in 1976, Embry worked briefly for the center as an interviewer and assisted with the Utah labor oral history project. Eugene Campbell suggested she start another project interviewing the children of plural marriages sanctioned by The Church of Jesus Christ of Latter-day Saints in the latter-half of the nineteenth century but disallowed after the 1890 Manifesto. Embry continued the LDS Polygamy Oral History Project after she was hired as director and started the LDS Family Life Oral History Project as a basis for comparing polygamous and monogamous families.

In 1974, Professor G. Wesley Johnson of the University of California, Santa Barbara, taught a seminar on family and public history. Johnson felt the class of twenty students was so successful that he hoped to do a family history symposium at BYU. Although the symposium did not occur, the history department later hired Johnson to develop a public history program. The center also tried unsuccessfully to hire Tamara Harevan, a prominent demographer. After the first two summers, the history department decided not to fund a visiting scholar for a time.

Board members suggested the center sponsor lectures or symposiums. In 1972, the Redd Center and the Festival of Mormon Arts invited architect Fred Markham and artist Dale Fletcher as guest speakers. Because of poor attendance, the center decided to sponsor its own lectures. Arrington recorded the following in his diary on September 28, 1972: "Yesterday the Charles Redd Center for Western Studies at Brigham Young University held the inaugural lecture in its Charles Redd Lectures on the American West series." Dr. Clark Spence of the University of Illinois spoke about livery stables. Before his lecture began in the Martin Life Science Center, Dean "Martin Hickman wheeled in Charlie and Anna Lee [sic] was with him. Everybody applauded as he was wheeled in." He noted, "Charlie very obviously enjoyed it very much." Arrington also held up the first Redd Center monograph by Gene M. Gressley entitled *West by East: The American West in the Gilded Age* for the 150 lecture attendees to see and applaud.[17]

At first, the directors suggested an ambitious yearly lecture series, but in 1974, the university administration suggested the center only have five lectures a year. The first year, the center directors felt they could only afford one outside lecturer, so most speakers were BYU faculty. The next school year, the directors planned five lectures, including one by Yale University historian Howard Lamar, partially funded by a grant from the Utah Endowment for the Humanities. BYU Radio taped the talks for network syndication. The 1976–77 lectures focused on Utah and the Mountain West, and the center invited University of New Mexico historian Gerald Nash. In 1978, the center sponsored dialogues on issues relating to the American West. They published the early lectures as short Charles Redd Center monographs.

From the beginning, a recurring issue burdened the board: how to pay for the center's programs. While Charlie and Annaley Redd gave a sizable grant to BYU, not all of the money materialized at the beginning, and the center's ambitious plans exceeded its initial funding. In 1974, Arrington suggested creating a business advisory board for fundraising, but most of the effort fell upon Alexander, who worked very hard to receive clearance from the BYU development office to contact donors. Since Alexander estimated the interest on Redd contribution would produce about $40,000 a year, he hoped to raise another $500,000 from friends of the Redd family. Unfortunately, these fundraising efforts failed. Despite these limitations, the center held lectures, published books, invited and housed visiting scholars, started an oral history program, and sponsored scholarships.

For the first eight years, Arrington directed the Redd Center and held the Lemuel Hardison Redd Jr. Chair of Western History. During that time, he also worked as church historian and later as director of the Church Historical Office. Alexander worked closely with Arrington in making decisions for the center, but Alexander ran the daily operations. On two separate occasions, Arrington recorded in his journal that he felt Alexander should direct the center.[18] Arrington, however, continued to serve as director until church leaders relocated the Church History Division to BYU. Arrington's name added prestige to the center. In the meantime, Alexander became a well-known western historian in his own right. On March 10, 1977, Arrington recorded in his diary, "I'll make a major effort to resign as director of the Redd Center. I tried this in 1973, to no effect. But perhaps I would be more successful today. I would still retain the Redd professorship, simply as something to fall back upon if I am ever released here. While the Redd Center does not take much time (Tom [Alexander] does most of the work), it does take some time, and I think it would be better administered by Tom alone than by Tom always having to refer matters to me."[19]

Alexander had indeed been doing the bulk of the work since the center's inception. He wrote a brief center history in 1973, in which he outlined the goals for the Redd Center. Plans included continuing the monograph and lecture series. Alexander supported a program for statewide oral history; suggested the Redd Center provide topics for dissertations; and initiated funding research grants to PhD students, faculty, and senior scholars. He believed the Redd Center's main emphasis should be to support research. Alexander was also especially interested in documenting a history of Charlie Redd, which the family later asked Arrington to write.[20]

One of Arrington's last notes about the Redds in his diary was on January 26, 1988. "Saturday, July 23, Harriet and I drove at 3 pm to La Sal, Utah. We had been invited by Hardy and Sunny Redd, who, with [their mother/in-law] Annaley, were hosting their family to a semi-annual meeting of the Charles Redd Foundation, and to a family get-together. . . . Spent a couple of hours on the porch talking with the Redds about [their deceased father/husband] Charlie." They toured the ranch in Paradox Valley, Colorado, owned and managed by Charlie's son Paul, before returning to the big white house for a feast at the "big table." Arrington commented how much he appreciated the hospitality of the Redd family to him through the years.[21]

Arrington eventually had an opportunity to repay the Redds' kindness to him and their financial support of the Redd Center and Redd endowed chair. Charlie and An-naley's oldest son, Hardy, commissioned Arrington to write a biography of his father. Arrington's *Charlie Redd: Utah's Audacious Stockman* was published in 1995, chronicling the life of this Utah cattleman and sheep grower from southeaster Utah.[22] Arrington noted "As the first occupant of the Lemuel H. Redd Chair of Western History at Brigham Young University, which Charlie established in honor of his father, and as the first director of the Charles Redd Center for Wester Studies at BYU, also established by Charlie,

Leonard J. Arrington

I enjoyed working on Charlie's life." He continued, "I had known Charlie for several years in the 1960s, and until his death in 1975, liked his sense of humor, his knowledge of and interest in Mormon history and culture, and his support of *Dialogue* and other public discussion activities." In 1964 Arrington received the first of Charlie's biennial $1,500 awards, given by the Utah Academy of Sciences, Arts, and Letters, for a significant contribution for the betterment of humankind in the previous five years in the field of the humanities and social sciences." Arrington continued, "Rancher, state legislator, entrepreneur, humanist, and philanthropist, Charlie built up one of Utah and western Colorado's largest livestock operations." He concluded, "Committed to traditional agrarian ideals of stewardship and to the value of the intellect, he employed both in striving to improve the conditions of cattle, sheep, people, and the land. He was an extraordinary rancher."[23]

During its first decade, the Redd Center mapped out plans to promote the study of the Intermountain West. Despite minimal funding, the center started programs to finance research, sponsor a lecture series, and publish a yearly monograph. In addition to the funds from the Redd endowment, the center initially relied upon grants from towns, the Utah State Historical Society, and the Utah Endowment for the Humanities to sponsor these programs.

The center's staff remained small, with Alexander and Arrington directing and administrating the center alongside a part-time student secretary. The university created a full-time position for Bluth as the oral history program director, but Alexander was not able to hire a full-time secretary. Two student secretaries were Pamela Campbell (Sua), who later became the social science specialist at the Jordan School District, and Deanne Whitmore, who worked all four of her undergraduate years at the Redd Center.

In 1987, the college provided funds so that the Redd Center could hire a full-time secretary. Barbara Lyman, Irene Fuja, and Natalie Ethington each held this position. Kris Nelson was the secretary for a few years, but she left when her youngest son was born. The Redd Center hired Olga de LaRosa, who worked for a few months and helped transcribe some Spanish oral histories. Kris decided to return to the work force, and Alexander helped change the position to half time with benefits. Kris remained at the center through Bert Wilson and Edward Geary's directorships, until her family moved to the Midwest. Director Brian Q. Cannon hired graduate student Jason Thompson as the office specialist. When he finished his master's degree, the center hired Mary Nelson. When she left the Redd Center to pursue cosmetology, Cannon hired Amy Carlin.

In addition to these secretaries, later called office specialists, the Redd Center hired graduate and undergraduate research assistants and oral history interviewers and transcriptionists. These students provided valuable research assistance. Those working in oral history made it possible to create a large set of oral histories. (See Appendix 7.)

1   Leonard J. Arrington, *Charlie Redd: Utah's Audacious Stockman* (Logan: Utah State University Press, 1995). Karl E. Young, "Charles Redd: Profile of a Renaissance Man as Rancher," in *Charles Redd Monographs in Western History* no. 5, *Essays on the American West, 1973–1974*, edited by Thomas G. Alexander (Provo: Brigham Young University Press, 1975), 106–31; Jessie L. Embry, ed., *La Sal Reflections: A Redd Family Journal* (Provo, UT: Charles Redd Foundation); "Charles Redd," BYU Redd Center, https://reddcenter.byu.edu/Pages/charles-redd.

2   Peter Novick, *That Noble Dream: The "Objectivity Question" and the American Historical Profession* (New York: Cambridge University Press, 1988), 583–84.

3   Daniel Ludlow was the first director of the Institute of Mormon Studies in 1961, and Truman Madsen became the director in 1966. The Religious Studies Center at BYU traces its origin to this group.

4   Leonard J. Arrington Collection, Series 4, Box 19, Folder 1, Special Collections, Utah State University, Logan, UT.

5   Arrington, *Charlie Redd: Utah's Audacious Stockman*, 234.

6   Arrington Collection, Utah State University.

7   Leonard J. Arrington, *Confessions of a Mormon Historian: The Diaries of Leonard J. Arrington, 1971–1997. Vol. 1: Church Historian, 1971–75*, edited by Gary James Bergera (Salt Lake City: Signature Books, 2018), 1:71–72.

8   Arrington, *Confessions of a Mormon Historian*, 1:103–04, 107.

9   Leonard J. Arrington, "Historian as Entrepreneur: A Personal Essay," *BYU Studies* 17 (Winter 1977):193–209; republished in Reid L. Neilson and Ronald W. Walker, eds. *Reflections of a Mormon Historian, Leonard J. Arrington and the New Mormon History: Essays by Leonard J. Arrington* (Norman: Arthur H. Clark Company, 2006), 84. See also, Gregory A. Prince, *Leonard Arrington and the Writing of Mormon History* (Salt Lake City: University of Utah Press, 2016), 78, 85–86.

10 Arrington, *Confessions of a Mormon Historian*, 1:97–98.

11 Arrington, *Confessions of a Mormon Historian*, 1:86n41.

12 Leonard J. Arrington, *Confessions of a Mormon Historian: The Diaries of Leonard J. Arrington, 1971–1997. Vol. II: Centrifugal Forces, 1975–80*, edited by Gary James Bergera (Salt Lake City: Signature Books, 2018), 2:332.

13 Arrington, *Confessions of a Mormon Historian*, 1:104n82 and 104n83. Henry A. Smith, "New Church Historian Called," *Church News*, January 15, 1972.

14 1973 Annual Report, Charles Redd Center for Western Studies.

15 Arrington, *Confessions of a Mormon Historian*, 1:626.

16 Arrington, *Confessions of a Mormon Historian*, 2:418.

17 Arrington, *Confessions of a Mormon Historian*, 1:299.

18 One of Arrington's New Year resolutions on January 1, 1975, was to "make an attempt to resign from the directorship of the Charles Redd Center for Western Studies, but retain my Lemuel H. Redd Professorship of Western History." Arrington, *Confessions of a Mormon Historian*, 1:783. On November 14, 1979, Dean Martin Hickman discussed Arrington's future at BYU. Arrington, *Confessions of a Mormon Historian*, 2:864. The Arrington papers at Utah State University include letters sent from Arrington to Alexander and Hardy and Annaley Redd on November 15, 1979, suggesting that Alexander direct the center and Arrington be appointed senior research associate.

19 Arrington, *Confessions of a Mormon Historian*, 2:358. On October 9, 1978, Arrington expressed misgivings that Elder G. Homer Durham and other church leaders intended the gradual liquidation of the Church History Division. Arrington, *Confessions of a Mormon Historian*, 2:651.

20 Arrington, *Charlie Redd: Utah's Audacious Stockman*.

21 Leonard J. Arrington, *Confessions of a Mormon Historian: The Diaries of Leonard J. Arrington, 1971–1997. Vol. III: Exile, 1980–97*, edited by Gary James Bergera (Salt Lake City: Signature Books, 2018), 3:532.

22 Leonard J. Arrington, *Charlie Redd: Utah's Audacious Stockman* (Logan and Provo: Utah State University Press and the Charles Redd Center for Western Studies, 1995).

23 Leonard J. Arrington, *Adventures of a Church Historian* (Urbana: University of Chicago Press, 1998), 232–33.

LEONARD J. ARRINGTON

Leonard James Arrington was born on July 2, 1917, to Noah W. and Edna Corn Arrington in Twin Falls, Idaho.[1] The third of eleven children, he was raised on a twenty-acre family farm that was a model of self-sufficiency. Arrington's father used a hand plow pulled by a horse or mule, and his mother scrubbed laundry by hand on an old washboard. On the farm, Arrington was responsible for driving the team, weeding, irrigating, and assisting with the harvest. He also got along well with the animals and cared for cows, horses, and his prize-winning Rhode Island Red chickens.[2] Although schooling was considered secondary to working the farm and completing chores, Arrington's father drove the children to school each morning in the sheep wagon, and Arrington actively participated in the Future Farmers of America (FFA) and the Boy Scouts of America.[3]

This academic support, however, did not extend to Arrington's educational aspirations at the University of Idaho at Moscow. Arrington's father tried to stress the importance of serving a mission to distract him from his studies in hopes that he would return to the family farm. His father was ambivalent enough about Arrington's studies that he refused to provide financial support for college but offered to pay for a mission. In the end, Arrington did not serve a mission, and he paid for his own education with scholarships and part-time jobs. His academic credentials and achievements as a state and national officer in the FFA earned him a scholarship at the University of Idaho. Arrington began his undergraduate studies in agriculture but switched after just one year to major in economics with minors in political science, history, and English literature. His coursework in the liberal arts expanded his worldview immensely and propelled him on to graduate school and an academic career. Despite the familial standoff between spiritual and secular learning, Arrington saw no disharmony between science and religion or his studies of secular and sacred thought.[4] After graduation, he pursued a doctorate in economics at the University of North Carolina at Chapel Hill. While pursuing his doctorate and working in Raleigh as a teacher, Arrington met Grace Fort, a lovely Presbyterian girl. The US army drafted Arrington in March 1943 during World War II. He was stationed at Fort Bragg, North Carolina, but received permission for a leave to meet Grace. Arrington arrived in Raleigh, North Carolina, where the two of them were married on April 24, 1943, followed by a twenty-four hour honeymoon before he reported back to Fort Bragg.[5] His first assignment was to a POW camp confinement center in North Africa where he processed Italian prisoners.

During this time, he read Dostoevsky's *The Brothers Karamazov* and, upon reflection, had a profoundly spiritual experience. Arrington received an impression that his calling in life was to engage in speaking and writing and use words as "heavenly messengers" and he vowed then and there to become a teacher and a writer about religion and economics. Later, Arrington was transferred to an assignment in Italy, where he quickly put his knowledge and skills in the field of economics to use working with economic reconstruction agencies. He also used the time abroad to learn Italian and acquired a proficient level of fluency.[6] After his discharge in 1945, Arrington worked to finish the doctoral program the war had disrupted, and his completed dissertation became the basis for his seminal work *Great Basin Kingdom,* a deeply profound work on Latter-day Saint and Utah history.[7]

During his doctoral work, Arrington accepted a position at Utah State Agricultural College (present-day Utah State University) and moved his family to Logan, Utah, where he and Grace had three children together and Grace was baptized as a member of the Church. Arrington's tenure at Utah State lasted until his appointment as Church Historian in 1972.[8] Arrington helped establish the Mormon History

Association in 1965 and served as its inaugural president from 1966–67. He desired a place where potentially controversial topics could be discussed. He supported publishing articles in *Dialogue: A Journal of Mormon Thought*. He helped establish the Western History Association and was elected president in 1968–69, was president of the Agricultural History Society in 1969–70 and was president of the Pacific Coast Branch of the American Historical Association in 1981–82. Among his other publishing accomplishments, Arrington was hired as Editor-in-Chief of the *Western Historical Quarterly*.[9] The family also took a brief sojourn to Italy where Arrington lectured in Italian on a Fulbright teaching fellowship.[10] Then, in the early 1970s, Elder Howard W. Hunter formed a committee to reorganize and professionalize the position of Church Historian. These structural changes led to the foundation of the Church History Department and in 1972, Arrington was offered the position of Church Historian.[11] Simultaneously, he employed his knowledge of western studies as the Lemuel Hardison Redd Jr. Professor of Western American History and director of the Charles Redd Center for Western Studies at Brigham Young University.[12] Thomas G. Alexander served as associate director of the Redd Center and ran the day-to-day operations, although he consulted with Arrington on major decisions.

In 1980, Latter-day Saint church leaders transferred the History Division—the primary writing branch of the Church Historical Department—to the BYU campus. The new center was renamed the Joseph Fielding Smith Institute for Church History. The Smith Institute assumed the responsibility of writing and publishing church history for members worldwide. Arrington continued as director of the Joseph Fielding Smith Institute for Church History until his retirement in 1987. The leadership of The Church of Jesus Christ of Latter-day Saints released Arrington as Church Historian and director of the History Division in February 1982 but the change was not even announced in April's General Conference.[13] Compounding this dramatic career change, on March 10, 1982, his wife of thirty-nine years of marriage—Grace Fort—who served as a pillar of resiliency and strength in his life, passed away of heart disease. The following year, on November 19,

1983, Arrington married Harriet Anne Horne.[14] Upon retirement, he continued to publish, producing a history of Idaho as well as several other histories and biographies.[15] Eighty-one year old Arrington died in his home in Salt Lake City on February 11, 1999, from complications due to diabetes and heart problems. Arrington donated his per-

Leonard J. Arrington

sonal papers to Utah State University and microfilms of his pre-1982 diaries to the Church Archives. The Arrington Papers at USU's Merrill-Crazier Library are extensive and represent one of the most significant archival sources on twentieth-century Mormon history.

Selected Publications

Leonard J. Arrington wrote many books, book chapters, and articles over his career, including twenty-one books on American, Western, and Mormon history and biography. He was especially skilled at teaching students and others how to research. While it is impossible to include all of his publication, this selected list includes some of his groundbreaking studies.

Arrington, Leonard A. *Great Basin Kingdom: An Economic History of the Latter-day Saints, 1830–1900*. Cambridge: Harvard University Press, 1958.

Arrington, Leonard A. T*he Price of Prejudice: The Japanese-American Relocation Center in Utah during World War II*. Twenty-fifth Faculty Honor Lecture. Logan: Utah State University, 1962.

Arrington, Leonard A. B*eet Sugar in the West: A History of the Utah-Idaho Sugar Company, 1891–1966*. Seattle: University of Washington Press, 1966

Arrington, Leonard A. *William Spry: Man of Firmness, Governor of Utah*. Salt Lake City: Utah State Historical Society and the University of Utah Press, 1971.

Arrington, Leonard A. *Charles C. Rich: Mormon General and Veteran Frontiersman*. Provo, UT: Brigham Young University Press, 1974.

Arrington, Leonard A., Thomas G. Alexander, and Dean L. May, eds. *A Dependent Commonwealth: Utah's Economy from Statehood to the Great Depression*. Provo, UT: Brigham Young University Press, 1974.

Arrington, Leonard A. *David Eccles: Pioneer Western Industrialist*. Logan: Utah State University Press, 1975.

Arrington, Leonard A., Dean May, and Femamorz Y. Fox. *Building the City of God: Community and Cooperation among the Mormons*. Salt Lake City; Deseret Book, 1976. 2d ed. Urbana: University of

Illinois Press, 1992.

Arrington, Leonard A. *From Quaker to Latter-day Saint: Bishop Edwin D. Woolley*. Salt Lake City: Deseret Book, 1976.

Arrington, Leonard A., and Davis Bitton. *The Mormon Experience: A History of the Latter-day Saints*. New York: Alfred A. Knopf, 1979.

Arrington, Leonard A., and Rebecca Bartholomew. *Rescue of the 1856 Handcart Companies*. Provo, UT: Brigham Young University Press, 1981.

Arrington, Leonard A., and Davis Bitton. *Saints without Halos: The Human Side of Mormon History*. Salt Lake City: Signature Books, 1981.

Arrington, Leonard A., and Susan Arrington Madsen. *Sunbonnet Sisters*. Salt Lake City: Bookcraft, 1984.

Arrington, Leonard A. *Brigham Young: American Moses*. New York: Alfred A. Knopf, 1985.

Arrington, Leonard A., and Susan Arrington Madsen. *Mothers of the Prophets*. Salt Lake City: Deseret Book, 1987.

Arrington, Leonard A., and Davis Bitton. *Mormons and Their Historians*. Salt Lake City: University of Utah Press, 1988.

Arrington, Leonard A. *History of Idaho*. 2 vols. Boise and Moscow: University of Idaho Press and Idaho State Historical Society, 1994.

Arrington, Leonard A. *Charlie Redd: Utah's Audacious Stockman*. Logan and Provo: Utah State University Press and the Charles Redd Center for Western Studies, Brigham Young University, 1995

Arrington, Leonard A. *Adventures of a Church Historian*. Urbana: University of Illinois Press, 1998.

1   Autobiographies include Leonard J. Arrington, *Adventures of a Church Historian* (Urbana: University of Illinois Press, 1998); Arrington, "The Founding of the LDS Church Historical Department, 1972." *Journal of Mormon History* 18, no. 2 (Fall 1992): 41–56; Arrington, "Historian as Entrepreneur: A Personal Essay." *Brigham Young University Studies* 17, no. 2 (Winter 1977): 193–209; Gary J. Bergera, ed., *Confessions of a Mormon Historian: The Diaries of Leonard J. Arrington 1971–1997*, 3 vols. (Salt Lake City: Signature Books, 2018).

  Biographies and tributes include Davis Bitton, "In Memoriam: Leonard J. Arrington, 1917–1999," *Utah Historical Quarterly* 67, no. 2 (Spring 1999): 176–80; Reid L. Neilson, and Ronald W. Walker, *Reflections of a Mormon Historian: Leonard J. Arrington on the New Mormon History. Essays by Leonard J. Arrington* (Norman: University of Oklahoma Press/Arthur H. Clark Co., 2006); Gregory A. Prince, *Leonard Arrington and the Writing of Mormon History* (Salt Lake City: University of Utah Press, 2016); Gary Topping, *Leonard J. Arrington: A Historian's Life* (Norman: University of Oklahoma Press/Arthur H. Clark Co., 2008); Ronald W. Walker, "Mormonism's 'Happy Warrior': Appreciating Leonard J. Arrington," *Journal of Mormon History* 25, no. 1 (Spring 1999): 113–130; David J. Whittaker, "Leonard James Arrington (1917–1999): A Bibliography," *Journal of Mormon History* 25, no. 2 (Fall 1999): 11–45; David J. Whittaker, "Leonard James Arrington: His Life and Work," *Dialogue: Journal of Mormon Thought* 11, no. 4 (Winter 1978): 23–33.

2   Gary Topping, *Leonard J. Arrington: A Historian's Life* (Norman: Arthur H. Clark Co., 2008), 17–19.

3   Topping, *Leonard J. Arrington*, 28, 30.

4   Topping, *Leonard J. Arrington*, 23–26.

5   Gregory A. Prince, *Leonard Arrington and the Writing of Mormon History* (Salt Lake City: University of Utah Press, 2016), 33–35.

6   Topping, *Leonard J. Arrington*, 39.

7   Topping, *Leonard J. Arrington*, 69.

8   Joseph Fielding Smith had served as Church Historian until 1970, succeeding David O. McKay as President. Topping, *Leonard J. Arrington*, 41.

9   Davis Bitton, "In Memoriam: Leonard J. Arrington, 1917–1999," *Utah Historical Quarterly* 67, no. 2 (Spring 1999): 176–80.

10 Topping, *Leonard J. Arrington*, 95.

11 Topping, *Leonard J. Arrington*, 101.

12 Leonard J. Arrington, Davis Bitton, and Maureen Ursenbach Beecher, *New Views of Mormon History: A Collection of Essays in Honor of Leonard J. Arrington.* (Salt Lake City: University of Utah Press, 1987).

13 Arrington, Bitton, and Ursenbach Beecher, *New Views of Mormon History*.

14 Topping, *Leonard J. Arrington*, 127–28.

15 Arrington, Bitton, and Ursenbach Beecher, *New Views of Mormon History*.

CHAPTER 2. THE ALEXANDER YEARS, 1980–1992

With the transfer of the Church Historical Division from the Church's Historical Office to BYU in 1980, university administrators determined that Arrington should not direct two centers. As a result, Arrington became the director of the new Joseph Fielding Smith Institute for Church History, and BYU officials appointed Thomas G. Alexander to take his place directing the Redd Center. Arrington retained the Lemuel Hardison Redd Jr. Professor of Western American History endowed chair, which altered the original plan that the Redd Center director would also hold the Redd Chair. This alteration made little difference in the center's day-to-day operation because Alexander had already been handling center responsibilities as associate/acting director for several years. Nevertheless, the two continued to meet occasionally to discuss plans for the center's operation.

During Alexander's first year as director, the Church celebrated its 150th anniversary on April 6, 1980, with a general conference session broadcast and President Spencer W. Kimball and Elder Gordon B. Hinckley delivering a "Proclamation from the First Presidency" issued from the Peter Whitmer Sr. farmhouse in Fayette, New York, where the Church had been organized on April 6, 1830. The Redd Center planned a lecture series on Latter-day Saint history and invited Indiana University–Purdue University Indianapolis professor Jan Shipps to present the keynote address. The series was one of the most successful in the center's history. Alexander and Jessie Embry complied these well-attended lectures into an edited volume. In addition, the center co-sponsored a three-day symposium with BYU Conferences and Workshops, as well as the anthropology, history, geography, English, art, music, and economics departments. This ambitious and very successful symposium included plenary and concurrent sessions on various aspects of Latter-day Saint history.

Even though the 1980 lecture series was very successful, others were not. The 1979–1980 annual report complained that audiences only attended when a topic related to The Church of Jesus Christ of Latter-day Saints was presented. Alexander expressed reluctance "to abandon the lectures" since conferences and lectures connected academia to the larger community, but he suggested that "even abandonment is a possibility."[1] When some board members suggested sponsoring symposia for scholars, Dean Martin Hickman asked the Redd Center to continue community outreach with public lectures. Even so, monthly lectures were discontinued in 1984 due to lack of participation. For example, the audience for one lecture in a large lecture hall consisted only of center staff and the speaker's friends and family. Because of poor attendance at this and other lectures, Alexander announced at the 1985 annual board meeting that the center would work with other departments rather than independently sponsoring its own lecture series. The sociology department cosponsored the center's first joint public lecture.

The Redd Center usually published the annual lecture series as monographs to reach a larger community. The center worked with the Brigham Young University Press to publish the books, and the library bought copies to exchange with other libraries. Alexander aimed to publish three monographs each year and insisted that "quality and scholarship should be sound" for each publication. When the university discontinued the press in 1981, Alexander arranged for Signature Books to distribute the volumes.[2]

Alexander also started a monograph competition to identify additional publication opportunities. The center advertised a contest to encourage authors to submit their manuscripts, and judges selected the best submission for publication, offering the author a small honorarium. The center covered all publication costs, while Signature Books distributed the books and gave the center forty percent of the sales price. Unfortunately, the competition did not produce many manuscripts, and the center shifted to consider submissions on a case-by-case basis. Even then, few authors participated. Alexander summarized, "I think that what we envisioned at first was a niche between articles and larger books. We could do things that were between maybe fifty and a hundred and fifty pages. But not a lot of western historians or people who work in western history are interested in writing those kinds of monographs, though. They would prefer to do articles that they can publish in scholarly journals or books that are published by scholarly presses. So a lot of what we published were the Annual Lecture Series that we had." When asked whether publishing practices were part of the problem, Alexander agreed that presses "have pulled back. You can't get a book published that's over about two hundred and fifty pages any longer. The presses realize that it's very expensive to publish a book that's larger than that and . . . people won't buy them."[3]

Alexander also encouraged programs that combined disciplines and resources. In 1979, anthropologist and board member John Sorenson suggested the center pursue a study on "the West as a human problem [or] the West as a colonial province." As Sorenson explained, "At first glance anthropology seems to have little to contribute to the study of the mainstream of development in the American West. Yet the broad, holistic approach of the discipline holds promise." He continued, "To see the past and present as a network of overlapping worlds in constant process of adaption contributes to a deeper understanding of some of the most significant events and settings which engage societies."[4] Sorensen hoped that the center would solicit federal government grants for environmental impact statements and other surveys. In 1980, the Redd Center board approved a five-year study of Sorenson's topic to create a database, provide scholars with office space, offer administrative and secretarial help, produce oral histories, and discuss the development of industry and boom towns.

From 1981 to 1982, geographer and board member Richard Jackson hired a Redd Center research assistant to work on the project. Possible other plans included a symposium, a $5,000 summer fellowship, and research funds. Jackson examined population changes in the

Intermountain West. Even though Alexander continued to promote Sorensen's project and Hickman offered money, few BYU faculty or Redd Center board members showed much interest. Pondering the program, board member James B. Allen said, "As you talked about that big project that John Sorenson was promoting, it kind of seemed to me like it could be almost an unwieldy project. In order to do it that way, you'd have to put a lot of manpower and almost focus only on that. I think if we want to be a center for western studies, there has to be some diversity in the kind of western studies we do."[5]

At the 1986 annual meeting at the Hole-in-the-Rock, some board members asked for a mission statement. In response, Alexander listed ten goals and their expected cost in the 1987–1988 annual report. Subsequent annual reports listed these same goals until 1992:

1. Student assistantships—$21,000
2. Interdisciplinary research study land and resource— $25,000
3. Annual symposium on American West—$3,500
4. Publish paper from symposium—$5,000
5. Funding for oral histories on minority groups—$10,000
6. Summer research for scholars and students—$5,000
7. Scholar in residence to research and teach one year—$50,000
8. Fully fund endowed chair—$1.5 million
9. Best book on the Mountain West WHA award—$1,000
10. Assist small non-profit entities hosting conferences—$2,000

After each goal, Alexander listed the year's accomplishments. During Alexander's time as director, he and Embry raised funds and developed programs for assistantships and oral histories of ethnic groups. These funding initiatives helped establish other programs such as monographs, new oral history projects, symposium publications, public programming grants, and increased endowments.

Alexander and Embry actively wrote and published books and articles during Alexander's term as director. Alexander's *Mormonism in Transition* (1986) had been slated as part of a multi-volume study for the Church's sesquicentennial celebration. He also published his award-winning biography of Wilford Woodruff, *Things in Heaven and Earth: The*

Life and Times of Wilford Woodruff, a Mormon Prophet (1991). Embry used the oral histories from the LDS Family Life Oral History Project in her book *Mormon Polygamous Families: Life in the Principle* (1987). As that project reached completion, Embry received permission to start the LDS Afro-American Oral History Project. The center hired Alan Cherry, a 1960s African American convert, to work on the project. He had published a short autobiography about his conversion to the Church and was anxious to research and learn about other black Latter-day Saints. He conducted interviews across the United States over a four-year period. Embry eventually published *Black Saints in a White Church: Contemporary Afro-American Mormons* (1994).

At the same time, the center sponsored numerous symposia. Alexander worked with the Mountain West Center for Regional Studies at Utah State University and sponsored a conference in 1987 on the impact of Leonard Arrington's *Great Basin Kingdom*. The daylong symposium took place at Utah State University, and speakers from many disciplines discussed the impact of the book in their fields. Alexander later edited and published these essays in a USU Press publication.

As part of the LDS Afro-American Oral History Project, the center proposed a symposium in 1988 to discuss the ten-year commemoration of the 1978 Revelation on Priesthood. Jessie Embry and Alan Cherry drafted a proposal for the symposium. BYU President Jeffrey R. Holland and Academic Vice President Jae Ballif reviewed, discussed, and approved it with sponsorships from the Redd Center; the Women's Research Institute; the Center for Family and Community History; the history department; the Joseph Fielding Smith Institute; and the College of Family, Home, and Social Sciences. The conference included an opening address by apostle Dallin H. Oaks, who presided over BYU when the revelation was given; comments by Redd Center African American Latter-day Saint interviewees; and a concluding address by African American genealogist James Walker. Approximately three hundred people attended the conference, including some Latter-day Saint general authorities.

In 1988, Yellowstone National Park experienced a disastrous wildfire, which inspired the center and the USU Mountain West Center for

Regional Studies to propose a symposium to examine the fire and its aftermath. The annual report stated, "Fire management has generated considerable controversy during the current year, and we believe that such a symposium under the auspices of the relatively neutral Redd Center could provide a forum for a discussion of the policy under favorable conditions."[6] The centers planned and sought funding for a May 1989 program, but the proposal was denied, requiring Alexander to cancel the event.

Other center-sponsored symposia included one-day programs on the following: Navajo culture (1990), funded by the Utah Endowment for the Humanities; a Provo City centennial symposium, oral history, and speaker bureau (1991), funded by the Utah Endowment for the Humanities; and World War II (1992), co-sponsored by the Utah State Historical Society and funded by the Utah Endowment for the Humanities. Many attended these informative conferences.

Peter Iverson, a well-known scholar of the Navajo Nation, spoke with other native participants in the Navajo culture symposium and an informal session at the end of the meetings. At the Provo City centennial symposium, speakers focused on Ute settlements and early Mormon colonization efforts. Embry set up displays about local businesses and architecture and worked with the Provo Library on an oral history project. The center hired student Jennifer Winn to train volunteers to collect interviews about Provo. The center also assembled a speakers' bureau to share additional information about Provo's history with community groups. These varied topics successfully engaged the public.

The World War II symposium invited those who fought overseas and on the home front to participate in the symposium's presentations. A German prisoner of war who was captured and sent to Utah talked about his experiences and his decision to return to Utah after the war. Jessie Embry set up displays with her father's uniforms and information about war-time practices. James D'Arc discussed World War II movies. A showing of *Since You Went Away* concluded the symposium.

The Redd Center continually sought additional opportunities to expand its influence. In 1990, the center cosponsored a Lowry Nelson conference with the USU Mountain West Center for Regional Studies and the Utah Endowment for the Humanities. The center also donated $250 to help the Women's Research Institute sponsor a conference for the 150th anniversary of the Relief Society. The following year, Alexander worked with Hardy Redd and Gibbs Smith to create a closed symposium wherein environmentalists and land users read and discussed their concerns, seeking common ground on contentious issues. The group met several times in San Juan County and Alexander felt that the experience encouraged friendship and built bridges that helped overcome misconceptions.

During his time as director, Alexander took two leaves of absence: once, when he directed the Washington Seminar, and again when he was commissioned to write *The Rise of Multiple-Use Management in the Intermountain West: A History of Region Four of the Forest Service* (1987). During Alexander's first absence, joint law and history graduate student Kenneth L. Cannon II helped manage the administrative work of the center. Professor Ronald W. Walker from the Joseph Fielding Smith Institute assumed the position of acting director during Alexander's second leave.

Alexander believed the Redd Center should promote BYU and the larger historical–humanities community. He served as a member and as chair of the Utah Endowment for the Humanities and sponsored some of its programs. He served on the board for the Utah History Fair. The center provided financial support to the annual fairs and funded special awards for papers and exhibits about the American West. Alexander endorsed the BYU history department's graduate program and helped find ways to invite quality students to study the West. He patterned the Redd Center assistantships and grants for students and faculty after those offered at other universities. One example is the internships Utah State University offered graduate students to serve as editorial assistants for the *Western Historical Quarterly.*

In 1987, Alexander requested additional funding for these student and faculty assistantships and grants from the Charles Redd Foundation, an organization which Charlie and Annaley set up for their children to meet and distribute funds to worthwhile causes. The Redd Foundation provided $63,000 for a successful three-year trial period.

Alexander wrote in the 1989–1990 annual report, "We think this is a valuable program because it supports the work of both faculty members and students and because it fosters a mentoring relationship between faculty and graduate students."[7] While the first assistantships promoted graduate students in history, sociologist Marie Cornwall requested that assistantship funding be available to other departments as well. Initially, only students applied for the assistantships, and after they were accepted, faculty members applied. Eventually, that changed to allow faculty members to apply and then they selected their own students to conduct the research.

Over time, the Redd endowment did not meet all the financial obligations of the Redd Chair and the Redd Center. Alexander approached the Charles Redd Foundation and asked the family to increase the endowment to one and a half million dollars. The Redd family generously offered to donate half a million dollars if the university matched their donation. William A. "Bert" Wilson, who replaced Alexander as director in 1992, convinced BYU president Rex D. Lee to match the Redds' offer. Additionally, Alexander became good friends with Karl Butler, whose mother was a Redd. Butler asked his sister, Hazel Butler Peters, and her husband Howard to offer half of their estate, which they had already planned to donate to BYU, to the Redd Center. Butler asked that the center create the John Topham and Susan Redd Butler Research Endowment. The additional funding the center received from these generous benefactors came after Alexander was no longer director, but his indefatigable efforts had a significant and long-lasting impact on the continued growth and vitality of the Redd Center throughout its existence.

The 1985–1986 annual report outlined that the Redd center sponsored oral history, grants for students and faculty research, research by the center, lectures and symposia, and publications. Alexander explained, "I believe that under the circumstances we are making good use of our resources for a balanced program of various aspects of research and dissemination of research." Alexander's years as director were remarkable because the center accomplished so much with limited funds while currently paving the way for increased funding availability for his successors.[8]

Leonard J. Arrington retired from BYU in 1987 and the university appointed James B. Allen as the Lemuel H. Redd Jr. Professor of Western History. Five years later, Allen retired and Alexander became the Lemuel H. Redd Jr. Professor of Western History. Because the director and the endowed chair were no longer synonymous, the university appointed William A. (Bert) Wilson, a folklorist from the English department, as the new Redd Center director.

Redd Center Directors Thomas G. Alexander (left), Brian Q. Cannon (center), and Jay H. Buckley (right) at the 2019 Western History Association meeting in Las Vegas, Nevada

1   Thomas G. Alexander, oral interview conducted by Jessie L. Embry.

2   Thomas G. Alexander, oral interview conducted by Jessie L. Embry.

3   Thomas G. Alexander, oral interview conducted by Jessie L. Embry.

4   John Sorenson, Box 2, Folder 2, Redd Center, UA 478, L. Tom Perry Special Collection, BYU.

5   James B. Allen, oral interview conducted by Jessie L. Embry.

6   1988–1989 Annual Report, Charles Redd Center for Western Studies

7   1989–1990 Annual Report, Charles Redd Center for Western Studies.

8   1985–1986 Annual Report, Charles Redd Center for Western Studies.

THOMAS G. ALEXANDER

Thomas G. Alexander is Lemuel Hardison Redd Jr. Professor Emeritus of Western American History at BYU. Born in Logan, Utah, in 1935, the son of Glen M. Alexander and Violet Bird, he grew up in Ogden and attended public school there. He earned an associate of science degree from Weber College (1955), bachelor's and master's degrees from Utah State University (1960, 1961), and a PhD in American history from the University of California, Berkeley (1965). In 1959, he married Marilyn Johns of Ogden. They live in Provo and are the parents of five children and six grandchildren.

The BYU Department of History hired Alexander in 1964, and he continued his illustrious career there until his retirement in 2004. Previous to that he taught at the University of California, Berkeley, and Utah State University. While employed at BYU, he lectured and taught seminars at the University of Nebraska at Kearney, Southern Illinois University Carbondale, and the University of Utah. Alexander served as assistant director, associate director, and director of the Charles Redd Center for Western Studies (1972–1992) and currently serves as a board member. Alexander is the author, co-author, editor, or co-editor of twenty-seven books and monographs, more than 150 articles, and numerous reviews. He specializes in Utah history, Western history, American Environmental history, and Mormon history.

Some of his books include *A Clash of Interests: Interior Department and Mountain West, 1863–1896* (1977); *Mormons and Gentiles: A History of Salt Lake City* (1985) (with James B. Allen); *The Papers of*

Ulysses S. Grant, Vol 5 (Asst. Ed., 1974); *Mormonism in Transition: A History of the Latter-day Saints, 1890–1930* (1986, 2nd ed. 1996; 3rd ed. 2012); *Things in Heaven and Earth, the Life and Times of Wilford Woodruff, A Mormon Prophet* (1991, 2nd ed 1993); *Utah, the Right Place: The Official Centennial History* (1995, 2nd ed, 1996, 3rd ed. revised, 2003); *Grace and Grandeur: A History of Salt Lake City* (2002); *Historical Dictionary of Mormonism* (4th ed, 2019) (with Davis Bitton); *Edward Hunter Snow, Pioneer, Educator, Statesman* (2012); and *Brigham Young*

Thomas G. Alexander

and the Expansion of the Mormon Faith (2019).

Alexander has won numerous prizes, including the David and Beatrice Evans Biography Award for *Things in Heaven and Earth*, the Mormon History Association Best Book Award for *Mormonism in Transition* and *Things in Heaven and Earth*, the Mormon History Association Best Article Award (three times), the Utah State Historical Society Best Article Award (twice), the Daughters of the American Revolution History Medal Award, the Award of Merit of the American Association for State and Local History, Phi Kappa Phi Emeritus Life Member, the Western History Association Award of Merit and Honorary Life Membership, and the Mormon History Association's Grace Arrington Award for Historical Excellence. He is a fellow of the Utah State Historical Society and the Utah Academy of Sciences, Arts, and Letters. At BYU he earned the Karl G. Maeser Distinguished Faculty Lectureship, the university's highest honor for a faculty member.

Professor Alexander has served as president of Phi Alpha Theta (the history national honor society); the American Historical Association—Pacific Coast Branch; the Mormon History Association; the Utah Valley Historical Society; the Utah Academy of Sciences, Arts, and Letters; and the National Society of the Sons of Utah Pioneers. He has served as chair of the Utah Humanities Council, the Utah State Historical Society, and the Provo City Landmarks Commission—along with committees for the Western History Association, the Organization of American Historians, and the American Society for Environmental History. Currently, he serves as parliamentarian of the Western History Association and has served as a member of the Western History Association council.

Active in his community and church, Alexander has also served as a Provo City neighborhood chair, as a member of the Provo City Landmarks Commission, and as a member of the Utah State Capitol Arts Placement Commission. In The Church of Jesus Christ of Latter-day Saints, he has served as a bishop, a branch president, a counselor in three other bishoprics, a stake high counselor, a stake and ward executive secretary, an elders quorum president, a high priests group leader, a Sunday school teacher, and in numerous other positions. He served a Latter-day Saint mission in the West German Mission (1956–1958), and he and his wife served missions in Berlin, Germany, (2004–2005) and in the Church History Library in Salt Lake City (2005). He currently serves as ward historian and as a Sunday school teacher.

Selected Publications

Alexander, Thomas G., and Leonard J. Arrington. *Water for Urban Reclamation: The Provo River Project.* Logan, UT: Utah Agricultural Experiment Station, 1966.

Alexander, Thomas G., ed. *The Papers of Ulysses S. Grant, Volume 5: April 1–August 31, 1962.* Carbondale: Southern Illinois University Press, 1973.

Alexander, Thomas G., ed. *Essays on the American West, 1972–1973.* Provo, UT: Brigham Young University Press, 1974.

Alexander, Thomas G., Leonard J. Arrington, and Dean L. May. *A Dependent Commonwealth: Utah's Economy from Statehood to the Great Depression.* Provo, UT: Brigham Young University Press, 1974.

Alexander, Thomas G., and James B. Allen. *Manchester Mormons: The Journal of William Clayton, 1840–1842.* Salt Lake City and Santa Barbara: Peregrine Smith, Inc., 1974.

Alexander, Thomas G., ed. *Essays on the American West, 1973–74.* Provo, UT: Brigham Young University Press, 1975.

Alexander, Thomas G., ed. *Essays on the American West, 1974–75.* Provo, UT: Brigham Young University Press, 1976.

Alexander, Thomas G. *A Clash of Interests: Interior Department and Mountain West, 1863–96.* Provo, UT: Brigham Young University Press, 1977.

Alexander, Thomas G., Richard D. Poll, Eugene E. Campbell, and David E. Miller, eds. *Utah's History.* Provo, UT: Brigham Young University Press, 1978. 2nd ed. Logan: Utah State University Press, 1989.

Alexander, Thomas G., ed. *"Soul Butter and Hog Wash" and Other Essays on the American West.* Provo, UT: Brigham Young University Press, 1978.

Alexander, Thomas G., Associate Editor. *Voices from the Past: Diaries,*

Journals, and Autobiographies. Provo, UT: Campus Education Week, 1980.

Alexander, Thomas G., ed. *The Mormon People: Their Character and Traditions.* Provo, UT: Brigham Young University Press, 1980.

Alexander, Thomas G., and John F. Bluth, eds. *The Twentieth Century American West: Contributions to an Understanding.* Midvale, UT: Charles Redd Center for Western Studies, 1983.

Alexander, Thomas G., and Jessie L. Embry, eds. *After 150 Years: The Latter-day Saints in Sesquicentennial Perspective.* Midvale, UT: Charles Redd Center for Western Studies, 1983.

Alexander, Thomas G., and James B. Allen. *Mormons and Gentiles: A History of Salt Lake City.* Boulder, CO: Pruett Publishing Company, 1984.

Alexander, Thomas G. *Mormonism in Transition: A History of the Latter-day Saints, 1890–1930.* Urbana: University of Illinois Press, 1986. 2nd Ed., Revised, 1996; 3rd Ed., Revised, 2012.

Alexander, Thomas G. *The Rise of Multiple-Use Management in the Intermountain West: A History of Region 4 of the Forest Service.* Washington, DC: USDA Forest Service, 1987.

Alexander, Thomas G. *The Forest Service and the LDS Church in the Mid-Twentieth Century: Utah National Forests as a Test Case.* Dello G. Dayton Memorial Lecture 1987. Ogden, UT: Weber State College Press, 1988.

Alexander, Thomas G., ed. *Great Basin Kingdom Revisited: Contemporary Perspectives.* Logan, UT: Utah State University Press, 1991.

Alexander, Thomas G. *Things in Heaven and Earth: The Life and Times of Wilford Woodruff, A Mormon Prophet.* Salt Lake City: Signature Books, 1991. 2nd Edition Revised, 1993.

Alexander, Thomas G. *Utah, The Right Place.* Layton, UT: Gibbs Smith, 1995. 2nd ed., Rev., 1996; Second Revised edition, 2003.

Alexander, Thomas G., and Doug McChristian. *From Arms to Aircraft: A Brief History of Hill Air Force Base.* Hill Air Force Base, UT: Hill Air Force Base, 1996.

Alexander, Thomas G. *Grace and Grandeur: A History of Salt Lake City.* Carlsbad, CA: Heritage Media Corporation, 2002.

Alexander, Thomas G., ed. *Times of Transition, 1890–1920: Proceedings of the 2000 Symposium of the Joseph Fielding Smith Institute for Latter-day Saint History at Brigham Young University.* Provo, UT: Joseph Fielding Smith Institute for Latter-day Saint History, 2003.

Alexander, Thomas G. *Brigham Young, the Quorum of the Twelve, and the Latter-day Saint Investigation of the Mountain Meadows Massacre.* Leonard J. Arrington Mormon History Lecture Series, No. 12. Logan, UT: Utah State University Merrill Library Special Collections and Archives, 2006.

Alexander, Thomas G. ed. *The Mormon History Association's Tanner Lectures: The First Twenty Years.* Urbana: University of Illinois Press, 2006.

Alexander, Thomas G., and Davis Bitton. *Historical Dictionary of Mormonism.* 3rd ed.; Lanham, MD: Scarecrow Press, 2008. 4th ed. Renamed *Historical Dictionary of the Latter-day Saints.* 2019.

Alexander, Thomas G. *Edward Hunter Snow: Pioneer, Educator, Statesman.* Norman: Arthur Clark, University of Oklahoma, 2012.

Alexander, Thomas G. *Brigham Young and the Expansion of the Mormon Faith.* Norman: University of Oklahoma Press, 2019.

Selected References:

Baugh, Alexander L., and Reid L. Neilson, eds. "Thomas G. Alexander: Interview by Dave Hall." *Conversations with Mormon Historians.* 1–32. Provo: Religious Studies Center, Brigham Young University, 2015.

JESSIE L. EMBRY

Jessie L. Embry was born in Logan, Utah, in 1952, the fourth child of Anna E. C. and Bertis L. Embry. She grew up in North Logan and attended Cache County schools. Her parents believed that travel was an important part of education. The family went "around the world" on the way to and from Iran.

After graduating from Sky View High School in 1970, Embry attended BYU, where she received a BA and MA in American History. She took an oral history course as a graduate student that influenced her professional career. She served a Latter-day Saint mission to the Canada Halifax Mission from 1974 to 1976. The Charles Redd Center for Western Studies hired her in 1979 as the oral history program director. Over the years, the Redd Center directors expanded her title to assistant and then associate director. During her thirty-five years at the Redd Center, Embry expanded the oral history program to include not only a collection of interviews but also publications based upon those interviews. With the support of Redd Center directors, she started programs in historic preservation, western studies, publication assistance to presses, and award programs to students and faculty at BYU.

Embry wrote or edited seventeen books and published over one hundred articles. Her books on Latter-day Saint polygamy, Latter-day Saint African Americans and other ethnic groups, and community and ward histories have been groundbreaking studies in those fields and opened additional research in those areas. She also taught Utah history; specialized classes in sports; ethnic, community, and religious history; the senior seminar class; historiography classes for the history department; and church history in the twentieth century for the Church History Department. Some of her students have become leaders in the Latter-day Saint studies movement.

Embry volunteered as executive secretary of the Mormon History Association for two four-year terms. She served on boards and as president of the John Whitmer Historical Association, as president of the Utah Women's History Association, and on committees for the West-

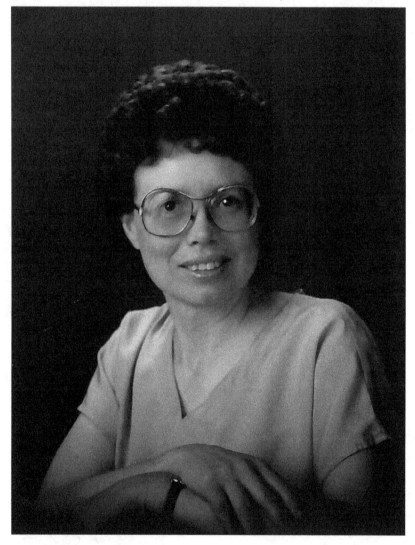

Jessie L. Embry

ern History Association and the Oral History Association. She was a member of the Provo City Landmarks Commission and served as a docent at the Church History Museum for twenty-five years. In 2004, the Mormon History Association honored her with the Leonard J. Arrington Award for a Distinctive Contribution to the Cause of Mormon History. The Utah Humanities named her a friend of the Humanities in 2002, and the Utah State Historical Society listed as a fellow for a distinguished career of research, writing, and service in the field of history in 2018.

Jessie saw her connection with the center as more than a job, or even a career. She donated her book royalties, payment for writing the Wasatch County history, and lecture honorariums to the Redd Center. She also promoted the center by publishing her books on Latter-day Saint ethnic groups through the center.

In 2014, Embry retired from the Redd Center. She has continued to actively participate in historical research and editing by volunteering as the editor of the *Journal of Mormon History* and as a research assistant for the historic sites division in The Church of Jesus Christ of Latter-day Saints.

Selected Publications

Embry, Jessie L. *Richardson Family History: An Oral History Study.* Provo, UT: Charles Redd Center for Western Studies, 1982.

Alexander, Thomas G., and Jessie L. Embry, eds. *After 150 Years: The Latterday Saints in Sesquicentennial Perspective.* Provo, UT: Charles Redd Center for Western Studies, 1983.

Embry, Jessie L. *La Sal Reflections: A Redd Family Journal.* Anaheim: Charles Redd Foundation, 1984.

Embry, Jessie L., and Howard A. Christy, eds. *Community Development in the American West: Past and Present Nineteenth and Twentieth Century Frontiers.* Provo, UT: Charles Redd Center for Western Studies, 1985.

Embry, Jessie L., *Mormon Polygamous Families: Life in the Principle.* Salt Lake City: University of Utah Press, 1987, 2009.

Allen, James B., and Jessie L. Embry. *Hearts Turned to the Fathers: History of the Genealogical Society of the LDS Church.* Salt Lake

City: Family History Department, The Church of Jesus Christ of Latter-day Saints, 1993.

Embry, Jessie L. *Black Saints in a White Church: Contemporary African American Mormons.* Salt Lake City: Signature Books, 1994.

Allen, James B., Jessie L. Embry, and Kahlile Mehr. *Hearts Turned to the Fathers.* Provo: *BYU Studies*, 34:2, 1995.

Embry, Jessie L. *A History of Wasatch County.* Salt Lake City: Utah State Historical Society, 1996.

Embry, Jessie L. *Mormons & Polygamy.* Orem, UT: Millennial Press, 2008.

Embry, Jessie L. *In Their Own Language: Mormon Spanish Speaking Congregations in the United States.* Provo, UT: Charles Redd Center for Western Studies, 1997. 2009 (Spanish).

Embry, Jessie L. *Asian American Mormons: Bridging Cultures.* Provo, UT: Charles Redd Center for Western Studies, 1999.

Embry, Jessie L. *North Logan Town, 1934–1970.* North Logan, UT: North Logan City, 2000.

Embry, Jessie L. *Mormon Wards as Community.* Binghampton, NY: Global Publications, 2001.

Embry, Jessie L. *Setting the Record Straight: Mormons and Polygamy.* Orem, UT: Millennial Press, 2007.

Embry, Jessie L. *Spiritualized Recreation: Mormon All-Church Athletic Tournaments and Dance Festivals.* Provo, UT: Brigham Young University, 2008, ebook.

Cannon, Brian Q., and Jessie L., eds. *Utah in the Twentieth Century.* Logan, UT: Utah State University Press, 2009.

Embry, Jessie L., ed. *Oral History, Community, and Work in the American West.* Tucson: University of Arizona Press, 2013.

Embry, Jessie L., ed. *San Juan County Public Lands, an issue of Blue Mountain Shadows.* Blanding, UT: p.p., 2013.

Embry, Jessie L., and Brian Q. Cannon, eds. *Immigration to the Far West: Historical Identities and Experiences.* Salt Lake City: University of Utah Press, 2014.

Embry, Jessie L. *Mormon Polygamous Families: Life in the Principle.* Salt Lake City: Greg Kofford Books, 2019.

Redd Family Memories: Jessie L. Embry

Jessie L. Embry was an undergraduate at BYU when the university announced the establishment of the Charles Redd Center for Western Studies in May 1972. She attended a lecture where a BYU English professor called Charlie Redd a Renaissance man. Charlie was in attendance, and Embry recalls that it was sad, as she could tell he had a lot to say but was unable to speak after his stroke. She learned more when she enrolled in the Redd Center's oral history class. It was fitting that the instructor, Gary L. Shumway, grew up in San Juan County, as Embry did her first interviews in that county.

Immediately after the class ended, Embry left on a Latter-day Saint mission. When she returned, she worked briefly for the Redd Center conducting oral history interviews with Utah labor leaders and children of Latter-day Saint polygamous families. Annaley Naegle Redd became an interviewee for that project.

Embry returned to the Redd Center in 1979, when Thomas G. Alexander hired her to direct the Redd Center Oral History Program. The previous program director, John Bluth, had accepted a position at the BYU library. Embry continued the LDS Polygamy Oral History Project and then created an LDS Family Oral History Project to compare plural and monogamous families. She hired interviewers and transcribers who followed her leads and talked to elderly people who remembered their family experiences. Over the years, she started new oral history projects related to the Redd family and San Juan County. The Redd Center and Karl Young had interviewed Charlie and Annaley's sons. Years later Embry interviewed some of the daughters.

Working at the Redd Center gave her a chance to interact with Annaley and the Redd children. Hardy Redd served on the Redd Center's board, and he asked Embry to interview people who knew one of the ranchers in the area, Marie Scott. For that project, Embry enjoyed a trip to southwest Colorado and learned a lot about the area. Later, Hardy asked her to help put together a volume on the history of La Sal. While Alan Cherry was proofreading the manuscript, he read about the bull sales and suggested that they go. Cherry, one of his friends, Embry, and her sister Janet drove to Paradox, Colorado, in a BYU car.

Along the way, they encountered some adventures, including a flat tire and having to take a longer route because of the Thistle Slide, a large landslide in Utah. Alan suggested taking chocolates to Annaley, which is how Embry learned that Cummings Studio Chocolates keeps index cards that listed their best customers' favorite chocolates. The next year, she suggested Alexander go to the sale. When he asked for an invitation, she had Hardy extend one.

Attending the Redd Ranches Bull Sale over the years was a way to connect with the Redd family and show them that the center's staff was interested in their activities. Embry has fond memories of the drive to and from Paradox. She enjoyed hearing Tom Alexander and Hannelle Wilson debate what a forest was as they drove through a national forest that did not match the definition in Wilson's native Finland. She remembers snowstorms at Soldier's Summit. She remembers jeep "traffic jams" in Moab. She remembers Brian Cannon's son asking why they went since it was a long way to go for a BBQ sandwich. But in the early years, they went to hear Annaley repeat a phrase Charlie had used for years, "We can have a bull sale because the Redd Center is here." Paul and Diane were always very busy with the sale, so they had little time to talk. But Hardy and Robert often walked through the pens with the center staff and explained the finer points of a bull sale. After lunch was served, Embry always enjoyed visiting with the servers, especially the Redd women, including Beverly, Regina, and Becky. Embry always enjoyed Annaley's beans and the beef that Becky's husband Brian Lambert grilled. Annaley's eyes always lit up at the Cummings chocolate. After Annaley passed away, the chocolates went to Diane, who also expressed glee and told Embry how Diane and Paul ate them as they relaxed after the sale. Tom Alexander, Bert Wilson, Ed Geary, Brian Cannon, and Jay Buckley have each attended the sale and made connections with the family.

Over the years, other Redd family members also served on the Redd Center board, providing a non-academic viewpoint. The Redds also hosted board meetings at La Sal and on a houseboat on Lake Powell. The family also worked with the center to help Annaley find new social outlets. Embry remembers going to lunch with assistantship awardees, Annaley, and other Redd family members. A sad memory for Embry was when Robert called and told her that his mother had died, and he invited the Redd Center employees to the funeral. Favorite stories she heard but did not experience were Leonard Arrington holding so tight to the rod bar on a Jeep over the Hole-in-the-Rock trail and Annaley allowing Alexander to help her in her kitchen because she considered him as family. She has stayed at Hardy and Sunny's home in La Sal and discussed canning and federal lands. Paul drove Embry and her sister Janet around Paradox to see the animals he was preparing for the bull sale. He taught Embry that even in a small town, one should never backtrack. When she retired and declared the Redd Center annual banquet as her retirement party, the Redd family members came and gave her a kind remembrance.

Working for the Redd Center was more than a job to Embry in part because the Redd family was so kind and gracious. In her opinion, they have been the perfect donors. They were interested in the center's activities and occasionally attended special programs, like the Hole-in-the-Rock conference and the cowboy poetry lecture. A few always made it to the annual banquet and attended the lecture. They did not tell the center how to run its program, but they were willing to continue to donate. Embry counted all of them as dear friends. She enjoyed when Kathy served on the board and asked about research related to her bookstore. Hardy was very helpful when Embry did San Juan County federal lands research. She enjoyed visiting Hardy and Sunny when Sunny was unfortunately in the Utah Valley Hospital long-term rehab facility. It was always fun to have an intellectual conversation with Robert or to visit the Dugout Ranch. Paul and Diane did an excellent job of running the bull sale and always warmly greeted everyone. Embry loved chatting with Regina, especially at the annual Redd Center banquet, and appreciated her updates on the bull sales. Embry enjoyed seeing Becky's quilts at the Springville art museum. Embry appreciated that Beverly was so kind to talk to and worked with the center on their grants. Embry enjoyed interviewing Maraley while attending a conference in Chicago. At the bull sale before Embry retired, she remarked that it was good to see so many family members and see they all loved the Cummings chocolates Embry brought.

The next generation of Redds are now serving on the Redd Center board and adding important insights. Regina's son Chester "Chet" served on the board for a few years. In 2020, Maraley's son Erik Rasmussen replaced Chet as the family representative. Embry has fond members of Erik stopping by to see Alexander when Erik was a student at BYU.

It is impossible to wrap up more than forty years of continuing friendship in just a few pages. These are just a few highlights of a very happy relationship that has gone far beyond simply giving some money to BYU.

Jessie L. Embry

CHAPTER 3. THE WILSON YEARS, 1992–1996

With Thomas G. Alexander's appointment to the Lemuel Hardison Redd Jr. Chair of Western History, BYU looked for a new Redd Center director. Alexander approached William A. "Bert" Wilson in the bookstore and asked if he would be interested in directing the Redd Center. Although uncertain about the decision-making procedure, Wilson responded that he was indeed interested in the position. Wilson recalled, "Not long after that they asked me if I would be the director. I had just stepped down as chairman of the English department, and having survived six years in that position, I figured I could survive anything."[1]

Wilson's years at the Redd Center proved advantageous—he was able to focus on the folklore archives and escape administrative responsibility in the large English department. During his time as director, he expanded the center programs and increased its ties to the humanities and folklore. Wilson hoped that the folklore archives would ultimately be combined with the Redd Center. He asked Kris Nelson, the center secretary, to input and catalogue information of student stories from BYU and USU into a database. Eventually, the William A. Wilson Folklore Archive waw incorporated into the Harold B. Lee Library's Special Collections.

While the center was multidisciplinary in theory and the board represented a variety of fields, the directors prior to Wilson had both been historians. As the new director, Wilson asked his colleagues and friends on and off BYU campus to serve on the board. These newcomers brought ideas for grants, monographs, lectures, and programs.

Wilson's appointment also gave the board the opportunity to revisit Alexander's goals from the 1980s.

For the 1992 annual report, Wilson listed these goals with the following notes from his first year as director:

1) Student assistantships—$21,000. Previously the Redd Center had given one assistantship for Sharon Carver to work with Alexander. There were not many applications.

2) Annual interdisciplinary research to study land and resources—$25,000. Wilson did not comment on this in the report, but he did explain that it was expensive and he was not sure where the money would come from.

3) Annual symposium on American West—$3,500. Alexander and Allen had arranged for Michael Malone, a well-known western historian from Montana, to give the history department's annual Swenson lecture. Thirty-five scholars of the new western history attended a round table and luncheon.

4) Publish paper from symposium—$5,000.

5) Funding for oral histories on minority groups—$10,000. Wilson pointed out that the College of Religion had given Embry a grant for the interviews and the center used its funding from the university to cover other expenses.

6) Summer research for scholars and students—$5,000. The center gave one faculty and three student awards.

7) Scholar-in-residence to research and teach one year—$50,000. While Wilson did not comment on this goal in the annual report, some members of the board felt it was important. Wilson recognized the interest, but he felt that having a visiting scholar would cost more than $50,000.

8) Best book on the Mountain West WHA—$1,000. Wilson questioned this goal because he hoped the Redd Center would be more multidisciplinary and not just give money to western history.

9) Assist in funding small non-profit conferences—$2,000. Wilson was very interested in this suggestion because he wanted to encourage public programming. He had served as a referee for the National Endowment for the Arts and knew firsthand how small museums and

art-based organizations struggled. Wilson explained, "I tried to bring that experience to bear on my term as head of the Redd Center to see if we couldn't be more expansive in what we were doing."[2]

His tenth and final point involved fully funding the Lemuel Hardison Redd Jr. Endowed Chair in Western American History, which required a financial commitment of $1.5 million. Wilson reported there was good news regarding the funding of an endowed chair. Alexander had already convinced the Redd Foundation to increase the endowment, but the members of the family wanted BYU to match their contribution. Wilson recalled that while BYU's development personnel expressed considerable doubts, Wilson convinced university president Rex Lee it would be turning down half a million dollars. Wilson explained the difficulties of persuading donors to contribute to an existing, named center, and Lee agreed to provide the matching funds to override BYU Philanthropy's reservations about the gift. According to Wilson, his discussion with Lee was "the day I learned that drinking Coke was a good thing to do because I was down buying Coke in the little market and he was down buying too." Wilson added that he was also in the same ward and high priest group as Lee. "We had a good relationship, and that helped too. It was the fact that he trusted me and we were friendly with each other. I wasn't just some cold outsider coming in and asking him to come up with half a million dollars for the Redd Center."[3]

During one annual board meeting, Wilson suggested, "We should let our imagination run free as we think about future directions for the center, but then we should rein them in long enough to consider how we could pay for the good things we ought to be doing."[4] In each annual report, Wilson asked the board members to consider how the Redd Center could help their research and discipline.

Wilson completed a self-study about the Redd Center in 1994. His description of its programs reflected his background and vision:

> The center operates from the premise that society is and will continue to be a reaction to or a development of our former societies and that by understanding the past we can better understand our present and prepare ourselves for the future.

In seeking to promote an appreciation and understanding of the Western American past, we take a broad view of the term "history." For us, the historical study tells the story not just of movers and shakers, but also of the common men and women who make up our society. And, while this research describes events and the development of social institutions, it examines also the reflections of historical circumstances in the arts—in literature, painting, sculpting, music, theater, film. While the Redd Center has traditionally focused on the past and . . . most of the work will continue to have a historical base, we are also very much interested in the present—in the way of life, the worldviews, and the social/cultural institutions of contemporary Western Americans. In short, we promote understanding of all aspects of the Western American experience, both past and present. And we do so with the conviction that it is important for our students and constituents to understand the geographical area that has shaped so many of their lives and for [Latter-day Saints], has played a major role in the history of their church.[5]

The rest of the self-study provided a snapshot of the Redd Center in 1994. There had been a downturn in the economy, so the center received less income from the endowment and had to depend more on the funds from the College of Family, Home, and Social Sciences. Even so, the center still paid half of the Redd chair's salary. Other programs included oral history, lectures and conferences, and research grants for students and faculty. The center continued to offer assistantships, fund prizes for the Utah History Fair, and publish monographs. Wilson added an oral history grant that provided travel and transcription services. When Marie Cornwall asked if the assistantships could expand beyond history, Wilson decided to include additional departments and allow undergraduates to receive the award. Wilson's English background led to the publication of Susan Howe's book of poetry.

Wilson introduced additional programs to the Redd Center. Because of his interest in museums, he expanded the public programming grants. He created independent scholar awards so that individuals without university affiliations could receive research assistance. Later, he changed the name to include creative works to show that the award was not limited to written research. He hoped to "encourage people and not just the best."[6] Wilson also revised the judging process for awards. The center asked three board members to review the applicants, but because judges came from many different disciplines, they often disagreed. One of the judges expressed concern that his top choice seldom received funding, so Wilson began the practice of awarding each judge's preferred application.

Wilson modified and changed Embry's title from oral history program director to assistant director because, with Alexander, she served as the center's institutional memory and managed its programs when Wilson had other responsibilities.

Wilson's direction included many other memorable programs. The Redd Center held a conference on ethnic Latter-day Saints where several members shared their personal experiences. The center collaborated with the USU Mountain West Center for Regional Studies in commemorating Utah's statehood centennial by funding the publication of a book about Utahns' views of the state. The Redd Center hired a student to help collect minority residents' stories. Embry received a commission to write the Wasatch County volume for the centennial county history series. The center did not plan any programs for the pioneer sesquicentennial anniversary, but Embry and Wilson researched folklore stories about the pioneers and published an article in *Dialogue: A Journal of Mormon Thought*.

In 1995, the University of Illinois Press needed funding to publish historian Ronald W. Walker's history of the Godbeites. Jan Shipps called Wilson and persuaded him to provide a Redd Center subvention to reduce the price of Walker's book. Wilson recalled, "But it wasn't just Jan that caused me to think that would be a good idea. I think the subvention for a solid scholarly work is a good idea. A lot of solid scholarly work won't always see the light of day without help."[7] Alexander supported that mindset: "I think the decision . . . to help subvent the publication of books probably was a good step for the Redd Center."[8]

As with department chairs, the college administrators established a term of three years for the Redd Center director, with the possibility of at least one additional term. Although the university did not officially reappoint Wilson as director, he continued to hold the position beyond his original three-year term until he retired from BYU in 1997. The Wilson years proved significant to the Redd Center in part because he helped secure additional funds that established its financial stability. He also expanded the center to include more interdisciplinary areas within the humanities. In the 1994 self-study report, Wilson mentioned that he hoped the center would work with any department that studied the American West, including "engineering, environmental, range management, forest, and mining issues." As Wilson left the Redd Center, he explained, "I appreciate the opportunity that I have had these past five years of directing the Charles Redd Center. It had been a pleasure to work with good people and to help increase the study, understanding, and appreciation of the American West."[9]

William A. "Bert" Wilson

1   William A. Wilson, oral interview conducted by Jessie L. Embry.

2   William A. Wilson, oral interview conducted by Jessie L. Embry.

3   William A. Wilson, oral interview conducted by Jessie L. Embry.

4   Redd Center Annual Report

5   Redd Center Self Study, 1994

6   William A. Wilson, oral interview conducted by Jessie L. Embry.

7   William A. Wilson, oral interview conducted by Jessie L. Embry.

8   Thomas G. Alexander, oral interview conducted by Jessie L. Embry.

9   William A. Wilson, oral interview conducted by Jessie L. Embry.

WILLIAM ALBERT "BERT" WILSON

William Albert "Bert" Wilson was born on September 23, 1933, in Tremonton, Utah, to Bill and Lucile Williams Wilson and raised in the small town of Downey, Idaho. Wilson admired his father's work ethic. He also inherited his mother's storytelling talent, which he developed throughout his life. Nevertheless, during his high school years he was an unassuming student who rarely cracked a book and spent his time before and after school performing manual labor for local farmers, businesses, and the railroad. Any hours devoted to schooling often ended in mischief rather than study.[1]

That all began to change when Wilson went to college. He was the first in his family to attend university and his worldview expanded exponentially when he began studying political science and Russian at BYU. He took a break in his studies to serve a three-year mission for The Church of Jesus Christ of Latter-day Saints in Finland where he fell in love with the Finnish people and Hannele Blomqvist, a convert of one year who was serving a mission in her own country. After their missions, Bert and Hannele married in the Salt Lake Temple and later had four children together. Attending BYU combined his thrill of intellectual inquiry with his knack at storytelling; nothing made Wilson feel more alive than rigorous academic work. Wilson abandoned his dreams of serving the nation as a super-spy in favor of following his love of words and stories. He switched his major to English and American Literature. He subsequently received an MA in English from BYU.[2]

Eventually, Wilson grew tired of the idea that only educated people could craft good stories and sought a more inclusive discipline. He found his niche at the Indiana University (IU) Folklore Institute where he earned a PhD in Folklore.[3] The "damned dissertation," as it was known in the family, was a nine-year project that would take Bert, Hannele, and their children from Indiana to Finland and then back to Provo, but they reveled in the distinctive cultural experiences of each place. His PhD research focused upon the folk culture of Finland; specifically, how the *Kalevala* was politicized as a tool for instilling nationalism.[4] During his time at IU, Wilson also collected word of mouth stories about the Three Nephites. Colleagues were astounded that he could collect Latter-day Saint folklore outside of Utah.[5]

Wilson's study of folklore helped him gain an understanding about many different cultures, but his later research into Latter-day Saint and western culture would provide him with a greater appreciation of his own. He went on to expand his initial research into Latter-day Saint culture to include everyday topics, and his studies have been instrumental in helping those outside the Church understand its surrounding culture.[6] The natural expansion from Mormon studies to western studies occurred when he spent the summer of 1978 documenting ranch life and culture in Paradise Valley, Nevada, for the American Folklife Center in the Library of Congress.[7]

In the mid-1980s, Wilson developed a vibrant folklore program and accompanying archive at Utah State University and began directing the Fife Folklore Conference. In 1984, he returned to BYU to build its folklore archive. Both collections began with papers students wrote about legends, beliefs, jokes, songs, and popular culture with Latter-day Saints or in the Intermountain West.[8] Wilson felt it was important to advocate for folklore as a field worth supporting and funding, as many university professors had a hard time believing that the stories, jokes, and traditions produced in the present could merit the same scholarship as works of art from the past.[9]

Wilson taught as a professor of folklore and Scandinavian studies and chaired the English department. After "surviving" six years as the English department director, he was asked to direct the Charles Redd Center for Western Studies and also became editor of *Western Folklore*.[10]

He worked to demonstrate a better concept of what it meant to be a Westerner, what it meant to grow up in the West, and what life in the West was like.[11] He approached editing *Western Folklore* with the goal that any articles accepted needed to be accessible to average university students.[12] Wilson believed that oral histories were the enduring contribution of the Redd Center and was filled with a passionate desire to research the folklore of the geography and culture that produced him.[13] He died on April 25, 2016, in Provo, Utah, after an extended illness.

Selected Publications

Rudy, Jill Terry, ed. *The Marrow of Human Experience: Essays on Folklore [by William A. Wilson]*. Logan: Utah State University Press, 2006.

Wilson, William A. *Folklore and Nationalism in Modern Finland*. Bloomington: Indiana University Press, 1976.

Wilson, William A. *Kalevala ja kansallisuusaate [The Kalevala and the National Idea]*. Helsinki: Työväen Sivistysliitto, 1985—A translation, with a new introduction, of *Folklore and Nationalism in Modern Finland*.

Wilson, William A. *What's True in Mormon Folklore? The Contribution of Folklore to Mormon Studies*. Logan: Utah State University Press, 2008.

Selected References:

Jamsa, Denise Wilson. "A Daughter's Biography of William A. Wilson." In *Marrow of Human Experience: Essays on Folklore by William A. Wilson*, edited by Jill Terry Rudy and Diane Call, 283–92. Logan: Utah State University Press, 2006.

Rudy, Jill Terry. "William Albert (Bert) Wilson: 1933–2016." *Journal of American Folklore* 130, (2017): 474–76.

Schoemaker, George H. "On Being Human: The Legacy of William A. Wilson." In *Folklore in Utah: A History and Guide to Resources*, edited by Stanley David, 78–85. Logal: Utah State University Press, 2004.

Wilson, William A. "In Praise of Ourselves: Stories to Tell," *BYU Studies Quarterly* 30, no. 1. (1990): 5–24.

Wilson, William A., and Frances Bivins Smith Rector. *Memoirs of William Albert Wilson*. Privately published, 1994.

1 Denise Wilson Jamsa, "A Daughter's Biography of William A. Wilson." In *The Marrow of Human Experience: Essays on Folklore* by William A. Wilson, ed. by Jill Terry Rudy and Diane Call (Logan: Utah State University Press, 2006), 283–86.

2 Jamsa, "A Daughter's Biography," 283, 286–87.

3 William A. Wilson, "In Praise of Ourselves: Stories to Tell," *BYU Studies Quarterly* 30, no. 1 (1990): 10; Jill Terry Rudy, "William Albert (Bert) Wilson: 1933–2016," *Journal of American Folklore* 130, (2017): 475.

4 Jamsa, "A Daughter's Biography," 287–88.

5 George H. Schoemaker, "On Being Human: The Legacy of William A. Wilson." In *Folklore in Utah: A History and Guide to Resources*, ed. by Stanley David, (Logan: Utah State University Press, 2004), 81.

6 Jamsa, "A Daughter's Biography," 288–289.

7 Schoemaker, "On Being Human," 81.

8 Schoemaker, "On Being Human," 83.

9 Jamsa, "A Daughter's Biography," 289.

10 Terry Rudy, "William Albert (Bert) Wilson," 285 and William A. Wilson, interview by Jessie L Embry, September 28, 2010, transcript and recording, Brigham Young University Charles Redd Center for Western Studies Redd Center Oral History Project.

11 William A. Wilson, interview by Jessie L Embry, September 28, 2010, transcript and recording, Brigham Young University Charles Redd Center for Western Studies Redd Center Oral History Project.

12 Schoemaker, "On Being Human," 82–84.

13 Jamsa, "A Daughter's Biography," 284, and William A. Wilson, interview by Jessie L. Embry.

CHAPTER 4. THE GEARY YEARS, 1996–2002

After Wilson's retirement, Dean Clayne Pope announced that Edward A. Geary had been appointed as Redd Center director in October 1996. Although Geary did not specialize in the American West, he was well known for his essays about, and history of, Emery County. Geary claimed, "It was through a series of unexpected strokes of good luck that I became the director."[1] Wilson had asked Geary to serve on the Redd Center board and suggested to the dean of humanities, Randy Jones, that he should appoint Geary as director. Geary described the situation in retrospect: "Randy was willing to do that, but he assumed that the College of Social Sciences [had] been picking up [Wilson]'s salary when he was the director. He figured, 'I can do a magnanimous thing that won't cost us anything.' He had a bit of a take-back when he discovered that that was not the case. Humanities would pay for me while I was here. But he didn't back out, so it did happen." In addition to his role as director, Geary also became associate chair of the English department. Geary credits his ability to fulfill the responsibilities of both programs to his capable staff: Kris Nelson and Jessie Embry. "The staff kept things really moving, so I just stayed around and did what [they] told me to."[2]

Geary continued most of the Redd Center programs, modified others, and started completely new programs. Hazel Butler Peters, a daughter of John Topham and Susan Redd Butler, requested in her will that half of their gifted property be donated to the Redd Center and to her parents' endowment. After her passing in 1995, the Peters estate was settled, and Geary hoped to use this additional money to start new Redd Center programs. His first priority was funding solid research. During the center's early years, award funds were limited, but by Geary's time, the primary limiting factor for awards was the quality of applications received. Public programming, however, was one area that received consistently strong proposals The center decided to fund exhibits and speakers for special events. Geary improved the process of evaluating grants by involving unbiased board members. Prior to this change, Geary felt it was a challenge for the board to make a collective decision. He described the issue as follows: "it's so eclectic that it's very hard to find competent judges or at least to get agreement from judges because they're likely to be more excited about things in areas they're interested in than others."[3]

Geary initiated plans to support newer, younger BYU professors. At the end of the twentieth century, university administration developed a new program to promote faculty research in two categories: senior scholars and young scholars (faculty who had been at the university for less than ten years). Geary worked with BYU to create a professorship for western studies. Geary commented on the fortuitous teamwork with university administration to encourage interest in western studies and make research in that field more available to faculty. While discussing the results of this initiative, Geary said, "You really do get a significant return. The young scholars get support at a crucial time that enables them to get their work out and going. The center [also] gets associated with some creative force in Western American Studies."[4] Geary took special interest in these young scholars, explaining, "I thought that senior scholars were already well launched. They would enjoy getting an award, but it probably wouldn't make much difference in what they're doing. For the young scholar it might make a difference."[5] Additionally, the cost of fellowshipping a young scholar was about half the cost of sponsoring senior scholars, making it easier to work into the Redd Center's budget.

Thomas G. Alexander believed that the center should sponsor small group seminars and help young scholars. He talked to Geary and developed a workshop for recent PhD graduates to develop their dissertations into books. Geary agreed to allocate $15,000 and the College of Family, Home, and Social Sciences agreed to pay any additional costs incurred. Alexander invited two western scholars, Richard Etulain and Glenda Riley, to help the students. The Redd Center put out a call for applicants and ultimately invited six students to attend the workshop. Alexander and the participants were very pleased with the results, but both the college and Geary felt that it was too expensive to be repeated.

Geary created a Western American Studies minor with the goal to "elevate our profile within the university."[6] This new minor provided educational opportunities to students who may not have recognized their interest in the West before. As a newly formalized field of study at BYU, it drew upon western American interests in a variety of departments across campus. University policy stated that academic programs must be housed in academic departments, and since the Redd Center was never a department with academic programs, the Western American Studies minor became part of the American Studies program. Due to the interdisciplinary approach of western studies, selecting American Studies as its home base was a "practical decision." The Redd Center and the American Studies program selected existing classes to establish required and elective courses for the minor. The center agreed to offer an introductory class, American Studies 200, "with the idea that you've got to get people into this before you can do much with them."[7] The course was offered for the first time in 1998, taught by Embry.

The Redd Center continued to struggle with attendance at lectures. In 1998, Geary decided the center should sponsor only two lectures a year, one by a BYU professor and one by an off-campus speaker. Geary named these lectures after their donors—Annaley Naegle Redd and William Howard and Hazel Butler Peters—so that Annaley received more recognition and the Peters family were acknowledged for their monetary donation.

In March 2000, the center sponsored a conference on the spiritual frontiers in western American literature. The three-day conference had sessions at the Marriott Hotel in Provo and on BYU campus and included a bus tour to Park City. Environmentalist Terry Tempest Williams gave the closing banquet presentation.

The center worked with the University of Colorado Boulder to provide information to Patricia Limerick and William Riebsame on a proposed *Handbook for the New West*. Although Limerick and Riebsame could not attend, board members, BYU faculty, Redd family members, and friends attended a dinner and answered questions about the New West.

The Redd Center also added some new awards for organizations. Alexander collaborated with the Western History Association to fund an award for the best article in religious history on the West. The prize was named for two active members in the organization: Leonard J. Arrington and Francis Prucha, a Catholic father. David Magleby arranged funding for the best paper presented at the Western Political Science Association. Steven Olson arranged for the best exhibit in the area presented by the Western Museum Association. Embry was active in the Coalition of Western Historians and offered to have the Redd Center pay for the annual Jensen-Miller award for women's history. The Redd Center negotiated with the Western American Literature Association and agreed to fund a public programming grant each year for a speaker at the annual convention.

As the internet became a popular and important tool for publicity and research, the Redd Center recognized the need to create an online presence. Kris Nelson designed and published the first center webpage,

Edward A. Geary

which described the center's activities, awards, and upcoming events. The center used this website to advertise their 2000–2001 press publication subvention program. The center offered to fund up to $3,000 to reduce the purchase price per book or to add illustration while keeping the sale price low.

Geary decided to leave the Redd Center in 2002 to accept

a position as the English department chair. Geary explained, "I was responding to a personal plea from a friend, essentially. John Tanner felt that the English department was at a crucial moment and thought there were some things that I could contribute."[8]

Summary

For Geary, one highlight of directorship was his office location in the Harold B. Lee Library. He said, "That was a kind of magnificent retreat for me." With the emergence of additional funding, many new programs—professorships and faculty scholarships, awards for conferences and other organizations, and the Western American Studies minor—became noteworthy trademarks of the Redd Center. Geary fondly recalled the accomplishments of the center as follows: "Again, as with everything, I think you look at the legacy in terms of individuals whose work was fostered, whose minds were stretched or focused and enriched in some way. That's the hardest legacy to measure, but I think it is by far the most important legacy."[9]

1   Edward A. Geary, oral interview conducted by Jessie L. Embry.
2   Edward A. Geary, oral interview conducted by Jessie L. Embry.
3   Edward A. Geary, oral interview conducted by Jessie L. Embry.
4   Edward A. Geary, oral interview conducted by Jessie L. Embry.
5   Edward A. Geary, oral interview conducted by Jessie L. Embry.
6   Edward A. Geary, oral interview conducted by Jessie L. Embry.
7   Edward A. Geary, oral interview conducted by Jessie L. Embry.
8   Edward A. Geary, oral interview conducted by Jessie L. Embry.
9   Edward A. Geary, oral interview conducted by Jessie L. Embry.

EDWARD A. GEARY

Edward Acord Geary is a product of Utah's "arid quarter"—the ragged horizons and abrupt canyons, the long views, crystalline light, and dry tang of the air on the Colorado Plateau—where he was born in 1937. Geary grew up in the town of Huntington in a close-knit neighborhood with grandparents, aunts and uncles, and cousins near at hand. He is descended from a long line of taciturn Edward Gearys, reaching back to the English Midlands and filling a section of the churchyard at Thornton, Leicestershire. His middle name came from a maternal great-uncle who starred in numerous B-grade silent Westerns and was memorialized by John Wayne as "the toughest SOB" of all the Hollywood cowboys. Geary grew up on family stories and developed early the fascination with connections in place and time that are the subject matter of most of his published work.

After graduating from North Emery High School in 1956, Geary attended Carbon College, in Price, where his father taught speech and drama, then went to BYU where he earned BA and MA degrees in English in 1960 and 1963. He completed a PhD in English Literature at Stanford University in 1971. He joined the BYU English department in 1968 and continued until his retirement in 2006, serving terms as graduate coordinator, associate chair, and department chair. He served as editor of *BYU Studies* (1983–91), associate dean of the College of Humanities (1993–97), and director of the Charles Redd Center for Western Studies (1997–2003). He also served on the Board of Directors of the Utah Arts Council (1985–93) and chaired the Utah Centennial County History

Council (1992–96). In retirement, he is a member of the Emery County Public Lands Council (2009–) and chairs the Emery County Historic Preservation Commission (2012–). He has been on the National Board for the Evans Biography Award since 2001.

In addition to articles in literary history and criticism in British, American, and Mormon regional literature, Geary has published three books with a regional emphasis: *Goodbye to Poplarhaven: Recollections of a Utah Boyhood* (1992), *The Proper Edge of the Sky: The High Plateaus of Utah* (1992), and *A History of Emery County* (1996). He was honored with the Charles Redd Humanities Prize of the Utah Academy of Sciences, Arts, and Letters (1994); the Morris S. Rosenblatt Award (1985) and the Dale L. Morgan Award (1999) from the *Utah Historical Quarterly*; and a Certificate of Commendation from the American Association for State and Local History (1994).

My Years with the Redd Center: Edward A. Geary

Geary's grandfather was personally acquainted with Charlie Redd. The same claim could be made for any number of livestock operators, big and small, across a wide swath of Utah and Colorado. Charlie was a gregarious and a canny businessman who maintained an acquaintance with most of the men he had dealings with. Geary remembered a story told by Charlie's son Hardy years ago: Hardy was driving his dad somewhere in Wayne County when they passed a man driving cattle along the road. Charlie pronounced a name and told Hardy to stop the car. After a conference on the side of the road lasting several minutes, Charlie returned to the car and reported that he had been mistaken about the man's identity, but they had nevertheless had a good visit and Charlie had persuaded the man to come to the next bull sale.

Geary remembered one of the bulls his grandpa bought from the Redd Ranches, an animal of unreliable temperament but excellent conformation, with a dark red coat (red with a double *d*!) that Geary thought looked much better than the orange-red of most Herefords. Geary raised two good stock-show steers sired by the Redd bull while Geary was in his teens. Geary also listened eagerly to his grandpa's description of the ranch at La Sal, which sounded exactly like the kind of place Geary would like to own someday. Years later, Geary discovered that while La

Sal was indeed a very nice place, the true platonic ideal of cattle ranches is the Dugout, developed by Charlie's rival, Al Scorup.

In the early 1980s, Geary participated in a Redd Center lecture series celebrating the sesquicentennial of The Church of Jesus Christ of Latter-day Saints and another series on community development in the American West. These lectures and the resulting volumes represented his first opportunity to work with Jessie L. Embry, who would be closely associated with his later service at the Redd Center. He joined the center advisory council in 1992 because of Director William A. "Bert" Wilson's efforts to broaden the center's disciplinary reach. In 1997, Geary succeeded Wilson as the second director not trained in history.

Geary remembered his five years in the Redd Center with great fondness. Wilson's term was dominated by a campaign to strengthen the center's finances. He worked persistently and effectively with university and college administrations, as well as with the Redd family to build the Lemuel H. Redd endowment to the point where it could adequately reflect the donors' intentions. Geary assumed the directorship as similar arrangements for the John and Susan Redd Butler endowment were being implemented. This greatly improved the center's operating budget, as the earnings from the Lemuel H. Redd endowment went primarily to support the professorship. This enabled the center to expand research awards and grants, establish lectureships, and explore cooperative awards arrangements with several professional organizations in western studies. This expansion of the Redd Center's activities has continued and increased under subsequent directors.

Looking back, Geary recollected that directing the Charles Redd Center was probably the best job he ever had—certainly the best administrative job. Seated by the big window in the spacious Redd Center quarters on the fourth floor of the library, with a magnificent Navajo weaving on his wall, and with Embry hard at work in the next office, he felt he had all he could wish for and more than he deserved. Geary loved the annual bull sales (always, it seemed, on the windiest day of April), the opportunity to become acquainted with the remarkable Annaley Redd and several members of her family, and with the remarkable Karl Butler. Geary loved the advisory board meeting they convened at the La Sal ranch, with side trips to Paradox and Indian Creek. He counted his association with the Redd Center as one of the highlights of his life.

Selected Publications

Geary, Edward A. A *History of Emery County*. Utah Centennial County History Series. Salt Lake City: Utah State Historical Society, 1996.

Geary, Edward A. *The Proper Edge of the Sky: The High Plateaus of Utah*. Salt Lake City: University of Utah Press, 1992.

Geary, Edward A. *Goodbye to Poplarhaven: Recollections of a Utah Boyhood*. Salt Lake City: University of Utah Press, 1985.

CHAPTER 5. THE CANNON YEARS, 2003–2018

After Geary left the Redd Center, Dean David Magleby appointed Brian Q. Cannon as the director. Cannon, an associate history professor who focused on western agricultural history, had not served on the Redd Center board, but he had received grants from the Redd Center as a graduate student and later as a faculty member. When Dean Magleby offered him the Redd Center directorship, Cannon recalled, "He told me what he would like me to do in terms of serving as director of the center. He said that he thought it would be a chance for me to advance my own scholarship and, at the same time, provide some service to the university. So he billed it as a win-win situation for me and for the university."[1] Magleby was clearly pleased to have the center in the college and saw it as a strength and asset to the university. He expressed to Cannon his desire to examine other regional study centers and see if the Redd Center wanted to adopt any of their ideas or programs to bring more visibility to the center and the university. He knew that BYU would derive maximum benefit from the center if Cannon capitalized on the strengths of the Redd Center, combined with the ideas of other centers.

Although Cannon was appointed in the fall of 2002, he did not take over as director until January 1, 2003. Jessie L. Embry performed as acting director during the interim. Just three weeks after he assumed the position, an external review committee analyzed the Redd Center. Dean Magleby felt there was a direct connection between the Redd Center and the history department, so the same reviewers who reviewed the history department also examined the Redd Center's programs. Cannon worked very hard to learn all he could about the center, reading about its goals and programs and contacting past directors. He came into the interviews feeling prepared and confident that he understood the center well. Cannon took the reviewers' suggestions very seriously and tried to adopt the ones that made sense. Many of

Brian Q. Cannon

their suggestions matched Dean Magleby's recommended changes; as a result, Cannon had the support of the dean's office in addressing the reviewers' concerns and creating solutions.

In many BYU organizations, directors of centers and chairs of departments regularly rotate. Both positions typically serve a three-year term with one renewal. However, that formality, however, never occurred in the Redd Center: Leonard J. Arrington left the directorship because he concurrently held another position, Thomas G. Alexander remained as director until his appointment to the Lemuel Hardison Redd Jr. Professor in Western American History Endowed Chair; William A. "Bert" Wilson retired from BYU after five years, and Edward A. Geary resigned from the position. Cannon, however, served two three-year terms. Dean Magleby asked Cannon to remain for several addition terms because he was pleased with Cannon's leadership and did not see anyone else prepared to replace him. In all, Cannon served five three-year terms, the longest of any director.

Cannon prepared some strategy and planning process reports over the years that demonstrated his goals for the Redd Center. In 2005, he listed three goals and summarized the results:

1. Encourage and support scholarly research on the American West. The center gave $85,500 annually in awards. It sponsored two conferences, gave four article awards, and conducted eighty-seven oral history interviews.

2. Increase public awareness and appreciation for the heritage of the West. Cannon divided out the public programming awards and the museum award and listed them under his goals. He also supported the Utah History Fair, provided subventions for books about the Intermountain West, and funded public school teachers to attend professional conferences.

3. Expand and encourage the study of the West at BYU. The Redd Center sponsored four lectures. Embry taught the core class for the Western American Studies minor, the young scholar program continued, additional grants and prizes were awarded to BYU students and faculty, and Embry mentored oral history students.

Cannon created an updated strategy and planning document for

2007–2009. Cannon listed the same three goals and explained the associated plans. To encourage and support research, Cannon listed the same number of awards as the 2005 plan but added that he hoped to have "at least one symposium leading to a scholarly publication each year."[2] Plans were underway for the first symposium in May 2006. He later modified the goal to do a symposium once every three years. Cannon was also concerned about the lack of applications for the young scholar award and set a goal to advertise it more.

Cannon hoped to receive more applications for the public programming awards. To increase awareness and appreciation, he planned to increase publicity. Since the center listed the Intermountain West as its study area, he wanted the center to become involved in more states than just Utah. He wrote to state historical journals and asked if they would be interested in forming a relationship with the Redd Center. He arranged to fund an existing award from the *Utah Historical Quarterly*. The Idaho State Historical Society had eliminated the *Idaho Yesterdays* journal because of budget cuts, but a Redd Center board member attempted to save the journal through a co-sponsorship with Idaho State University, but the deal was never consummated and the journal did not survive. Cannon wrote to state history fairs and asked if they were interested having an award sponsored by the Redd Center. New Mexico, Arizona, Idaho, and Colorado accepted the offer. Embry judged at the Wyoming state fair one year and discovered why that state did not respond— they already offered many special awards.

Cannon came to the Redd Center at a good time, financially. Not only was there increased funding thanks to the Redd Foundation and the Butler endowment, the economy was also booming. Cannon had the luxury of funding more programs: He established a Mollie and Karl Butler Young Scholar professorship for BYU assistant professors specializing in western American studies to help further their careers. He expanded Director Geary's press subvention program and funded more research grants and assistantships than his predecessors. The one exception was during the 2008 recession, in which the university and college asked the center not to take a payout from the endowment because the stock market was so low. Fortunately, Cannon had not moved money from the spending accounts back to the endowment as the college had requested, so the center was able to continue to offer most of its awards during the economic downturn. Cannon's goal was to award $100,000 each year, excluding the assistantships.

Based on suggestions from an external review of the Redd Center, Cannon started the Western American Studies faculty luncheon to gather those interested in western studies twice a year. To encourage attendance, he arranged for an award winner, a visiting fellow, or another notable scholar to present the lecture. For Cannon, it was a good way "to promote collegiality and collaboration." Under Cannon's direction, this gathering evolved into a luncheon where a faculty member reported on their research. Cannon reflected, "I have pretty good memories of those gatherings. It's free food, but I think people enjoy the discussion too. I know when we had Bev Rhoder come in and talk, Phil Snyder said to me afterward, 'This is great. I don't get a chance to interact with scientists enough and to see what they're doing in the natural world.'"[3]

To encourage western American studies at BYU and recruit for the Western American Studies minor, Cannon created an American Studies class that capitalized on attending the Redd Center lectures and having BYU faculty such as the Redd Center's Mollie and Karl Butler Young Scholar recipients speak for a class period on their specialty. Cannon also announced a new visiting scholar program—a limited attempt to accomplish what Alexander had hoped from the beginning. Unlike the earlier plan to pay a salary, the new arrangement provided a housing allowance and an office for the visiting scholar. The Redd Center paid for a research assistant, a computer, and photocopying expenses.

The outside review recommended the Redd Center board include members from areas outside of Utah. Cannon was already thinking in that direction and appointed the first non-Utahn board members. Cannon also invited scholars from the humanities, social sciences, and biological sciences to serve on the board, including faculty from other universities in Utah, Nevada, and Idaho. These members brought new ideas and suggestions to the Redd Center. Cannon recognized the board members as advisory colleagues. He shared, "I see it as being advantageous for the director to be able to seek advice from the board. It can be advantageous in terms of going to administrators."[4]

Cannon continued the award categories but expressed some concerns about the center's impact. Although the public programs seemed to be an effective way to make a difference beyond the localized BYU community, Cannon explained, "The frustration there is sometimes you have to choose whether to support a small museum where your money could really make a difference, but the quality of the exhibit that's being produced is often less than a top notch display they would probably pull it off with or without Redd Center funds."[5] Cannon was especially concerned about the benefits of the independent scholar awards. "That seems to be where we get the smallest bang for the buck. On the other hand, I've been happy as time has gone on that we've had it because public history and supporting public intellectuals, as they're called now, is a very trendy thing to do. It's a sign that the center reaches out beyond academia."[6]

Cannon worked with John Murphy and the L. Tom Perry Special Collections to create a new category of grants that would encourage researchers to use the resources in the BYU Harold B. Lee Library. Graduate students and senior scholars received the awards, and Special Collections put up a plaque with the names of the winners. In addition to inviting scholars to visit BYU, Cannon wanted to encourage more BYU faculty and students to apply for grants. The Redd Center staff offered grant-writing workshops to help improve proposals. Cannon created additional categories for BYU faculty and students so they could be judged separately from faculty and students from other universities. Cannon also added an award of $300 for students working on their capstone projects to help with research needs.

The board suggested the center help public school teachers, so Cannon created an education award. One of the most successful examples was Julie Cook, who applied for funds to provide a covered wagon and books to fourth grade teachers in the Logan School District. Based on that success, the center offered the same materials to other teachers. Jessie Embry advertised the kit to teachers at the Rural School Association meetings, and teachers applied to receive the materials at the organization's next annual meeting.

Some board members expressed concerns that teachers did not have time to write grant proposals, so they suggested providing workshops and classes to the teachers. Embry presented at the Rural School Association annual meetings and developed a following with Emery County high school teachers, but aside from the year she offered wagons and books, very few attended. Embry presented workshops to fourth- and seventh-grade teachers in the Jordan, Washington, and Box Elder school districts. The board eventually decided the education grant was redundant and phased it out.

The teaching committee of the Western History Association provided another way to help public school teachers. Cannon worked with Brian Collier to create an arrangement for teachers to submit lesson plans for recognition and aid. Winners received a grant to attend the WHA annual meeting and the association waived the registration fee. The teachers then presented their lesson plans in a WHA session. The Redd Center offered a similar grant at the environmental history conference in Boise.

Cannon wanted to better advertise Redd Center grants, especially considering the center had increased funds available. The center distributed flyers to departments at universities throughout the West and commissioned Hales Creative to design a poster. Board members invited colleagues to send in applications, which proved to be a successful advertising method. Richard Jackson was especially good at encouraging geographers to apply. Cannon sent mailings to the memberships of the Western History Association and the Western Literature Association. He advertised the opportunities on H-West and other online announcement boards to spread the word.

Under Cannon, the Mollie and Karl Butler Young Scholar Award in Western Studies was established. At first, he proposed to offer the young scholar to just one college, or a group of similar colleges, so it would be easier to compare the accomplishments of the candidates. Initially, however, few applicants in the college qualified for the award in terms of the length of their BYU employment or their research interests in the West. After trying the selected college method for two years, the Redd Center opened the awards to all qualified applicants across campus. Sometimes the proposals were very different from one another, and finding qualified judges to review them was difficult, but the Redd Center invited scholars outside of BYU to examine the applications. The center temporarily placed the young scholar program on hold in 2009 due to the recession and lack of funds.

In 2006, Cannon explained to the board that Dean Magleby encouraged visiting scholars. To realize this goal, the board asked the dean for funding and suggested the college provide housing. The first visiting scholar, Julianne Newmark, finished a book manuscript and researched at the L. Tom Perry Special Collections. She later returned in 2014 for a second visit. The second visiting scholar, John Turner, worked on a book about Brigham Young during the summer and presented in classes. He also returned for a second term.

Cannon reintroduced Redd Center summer seminars, inviting scholars to write papers on a specific topic of theme. In the first seminar, twenty-one scholars participated, and sixteen of the essays were published in *Utah in the Twentieth Century* (Utah State University Press, 2009), edited by Cannon and Embry. Embry planned a second seminar in 2008. She edited and published the anthology titled *Oral History, Community, and Work in the American West* (University of Arizona Press, 2013). The third summer seminar resulted in the anthology *Immigrants in the Far West: Historical Identities and Experiences* (University of Utah Press, 2014), edited by Jessie L. Embry and Brian Q. Cannon. Additional seminars resulted in three more anthologies, including *The Earth Will Appear as the Garden of Eden: Essays on Mormon Environmental History* (University of Utah Press, 2019), edited by Jedediah S. Rogers and Matthew C. Godfrey; *Essays on American Indian and Mormon History* (University of Utah Press, 2019), edited by P. Jane Hafen and Brenden W. Rensink; and *Reconstruction in Mormon America* (University of Oklahoma Press, 2019), edited by Clyde A. Milner and Brian Q. Cannon.

Under Cannon's direction, the center sponsored fewer conferences but worked with organizations to promote its fellowships, awards, and grants. In 2004, the center co-sponsored a meeting of the German Association of the West—a one-day conference that brought in scholars from Germany who studied western American literature. One of the presenters, Thomas Jeier, gave a public lecture. In 2012, Douglas Major, who had been involved with the restoration of Bluff Fort, suggested an evening meeting about the San Juan Mission. Embry worked with Major and BYU Continuing Education to offer a session in the conference center that had "standing room only." A 2015 conference focused on Howard Egan's influence and accomplishments.

Embry planned an interdisciplinary conference to bring faculty together to discuss common projects. Board members Dennis Cutchins and Val Anderson suggested offering a $10,000 grant if faculty members created a project that crossed disciplines. The conference workshop provided an opportunity for BYU faculty members to "speed date" about their projects, an endeavor the Redd Center continues to support to help faculty collaborate on worthwhile projects.

Cannon was more excited about lectures than previous directors. "I would love to sponsor a lecture a month. The problem is the attendance. I would not want to be embarrassed by having no one come to the lecture. It's such a chore to go through the course catalogue and try to identify who the professors are who might give extra credit to their students. It's not really begging and pleading, but it is hard to always have to worry about that."[7] Still, Cannon appreciated the results. He saw the benefits of bringing in guest lecturers and exposing BYU faculty and students to different perspectives and research methods. Sponsoring lectures also helped meet some of Magleby's goals. According to Cannon, Dean Magleby was thrilled to hear about visiting lecturers such as Erica Bsumik and Phil Deloria.

Embry suggested that as the Redd Center looked for new programs to add, she could visit other western studies centers and explore their successes. Embry visited the O'Connor Center at the University of Montana, the American West Center at the University of Wyoming, the American West Center at the University of Colorado Boulder, the Clements Center at Southern Methodist University, the Southwest Center at Austin College, the Center for Southwest History at the University of New Mexico, a Latin American center at the University of San Diego, the oral history program at California State University, and the oral history program at the University of Nevada, Las Vegas. At the 2007 WHA meetings, Cannon participated in a panel discussing western American studies centers. The next year, the Redd Center sponsored a luncheon for western studies personnel at the Salt Lake City, Utah, WHA meeting.

The center continued to sponsor the Western American Studies minor even though few students declared it. Embry taught the American Studies 200 class until 2009. The class struggled after its first few years with a mixture of American Studies upperclassmen and freshmen. When Embry suggested the class was not servicing its purpose as an introduction to the minor, the American Studies program eliminated the class and combined it with the Western American Literature course. To replace the class, Brian Cannon developed a one-hour seminar class where BYU faculty and Redd Center awardees gave presentations about their research. This provided an opportunity for students to hear new research, as well as for the Redd Center to publicize its grant recipients and display the variety of western studies disciplines.

The Redd Center continued to provide funding for article prizes. During Cannon's tenure, the center added awards for Native American articles and a prize for the best book on the West sponsored by Phi Alpha Theta. Cannon also arranged to work with the Buffalo Bill Museum.

To connect historical research with modern appreciation, the Redd Center worked with an environmental group about the uses of public lands in San Juan County. The center conducted interviews with those who used federal lands for their livelihood, those who recreated on the land, and those who felt it should be preserved. The center published a small booklet with excerpts from the interviews and held public meetings in Monticello. They also held a writing contest to encourage county residents to express their feelings about the land. Community members and public-school students participated.

The Redd Center moved its offices twice during Cannon's time as director. When the Joseph Fielding Smith Building was completed, Dean Magleby wanted to combine all the college centers in a central location. Although the entirety of that goal did not happen, Magleby moved the Redd Center to the Kimball Tower, closer to college departments. The center was initially housed on the third floor, but the college remodeled some rooms and transitioned the center to the ninth floor in 2013.

Cannon recalled that when he was appointed Redd Center director, Alexander told him, "The Redd Center is very near and dear to my heart because I spent much of my career there. I care a lot about it."[8] Cannon continued, "That's something that's stuck with me and helped me to realize that people had devoted lots of time and concern and ef-

The Charles Redd Center at 954 KMBL (Spencer W. Kimball Tower)

fort to the center. It was a legacy that I was being able to share in now."[9] Cannon enjoyed his fifteen-year experience as Redd Center director. "It's been an opportunity for me to interact … with scholars and a variety of fields even if it's just reviewing their applications and seeing what they're doing. That's quite interesting and exciting. It helps me to see how anthropologists design research or how people in biology design their research, what they think is significant and how they defend significance. It's a chance to make some things happen on campus in a modest way. To give those opportunities to students and to see them get excited about it and to have them come back excited about what they found, that's a pretty neat thing."[10]

Dean Benjamin M. Ogles appointed Brian Q. Cannon as the new chair of the BYU history department in September 2018, which changed his administrative responsibilities and ended nearly two decades of excellent service as Redd Center director. In 2020, the Western History Association recognized Cannon for his outstanding contributions to western studies by awarding him the Gordon Bakken Award of Merit given for outstanding service to the field of western history and to the Western History Association.

1   Brian Q. Cannon, oral interview conducted by Jessie L. Embry.
2   Brian Q. Cannon, oral interview conducted by Jessie L. Embry.
3   Brian Q. Cannon, oral interview conducted by Jessie L. Embry.
4   Brian Q. Cannon, oral interview conducted by Jessie L. Embry.
5   Brian Q. Cannon, oral interview conducted by Jessie L. Embry.
6   Brian Q. Cannon, oral interview conducted by Jessie L. Embry.
7   Brian Q. Cannon, oral interview conducted by Jessie L. Embry.
8   Brian Q. Cannon, oral interview conducted by Jessie L. Embry.
9   Brian Q. Cannon, oral interview conducted by Jessie L. Embry.
10 Brian Q. Cannon, oral interview conducted by Jessie L. Embry.

BRIAN Q. CANNON

Brian Q. Cannon served as director of the Charles Redd Center for Western Studies from January 2003 to August 2018. Cannon earned his BA in American Studies at BYU, his MA in History at Utah State University, and his PhD in History from the University of Wisconsin–Madison. He accepted an assistant professor position in BYU's history department in 1992.

Cannon's early research focused upon American land policy, reclamation, and agricultural settlement, resulting in his first two books—*Remaking the Agrarian Dream: Rural Resettlement in the Mountain West* and *Reopening the Frontier: Homesteading in the Modern West*. His study of Utah and Latter-day Saint history resulted in a third book coauthored with Charles S. Peterson, *The Awkward State of Utah: Coming of Age in the Nation, 1896–1945*, which received an Award of Merit from the Utah State Historical Society. He authored dozens of book chapters and articles on topics including New Deal farm labor camps for Dust Bowl refugees, Great Depression–era documentary photography, reclamation of arid lands, the origins of the Church Welfare Plan, Indian voting rights, and American Indian indentured servitude. With help from Associate Director Embry, Director Cannon organized topical research seminars at BYU where scholars from institutions across the state and nation visited the Redd Center to workshop papers on common themes with the intent of preparing those papers for publication in topical volumes. These workshops resulted in six volumes prepared during Cannon's tenure, two of which were coedited by Cannon and Embry—*Utah in the*

Twentieth Century and *Immigrants in the Far West: Historical Identities and Experiences*—and one of which was co-edited with Clyde A. Milner II—*Reconstruction and Mormon America.*

By the early twenty-first century, when Cannon became Redd Center director, effective fundraising and endowment campaigns by previous directors and conservative budgeting had produced substantial cash reserves and a consistent stream of revenue, allowing the center to expand support for scholarship and public programming. During Cannon's tenure as director, the center inaugurated a visiting scholar program, enabling researchers to visit BYU to engage in extended research, writing over a term or semester, and increasing the center's professional footprint. The center's support of prizes and lectures for professional associations increased considerably, as did the number of research grants awarded each year.

The center expanded its support of state history day to states across the Intermountain West and cooperated with the Western History Association and the Western Literature Association in sponsoring scholarships to enable K–12 teachers to participate in those associations' annual conferences. The center also increased programming and re-

Brian Q. Cannon outside the JFSB upon appointment as Department of History Chair

search support on campus, expanded the frequency of lectures, instituted prizes for student papers and posters, offered interdisciplinary faculty research grants, and established the Mollie and Karl Butler Young Scholar Award.

Redd Center board member John Murphy was instrumental in helping Cannon establish the Charles Redd Fellowships which enabled scholars to conduct research for several weeks in the L. Tom Perry Special Collections Library. The center also instituted semiannual lunch gatherings for western studies faculty to promote interdisciplinary collegiality and provide a forum for faculty to present their research. During Cannon's tenure, the center's oral history program produced hundreds of oral history interviews under Associate Director Jessie Embry on topics ranging from Latter-day Saint sports and recreation to the Indian Student Placement Program, along with articles and monographs based on those interviews. In Cannon's final years as director, Assistant Director Brenden Rensink brought the center into the digital age, broadcasting lectures in real time to audiences beyond campus and creating *Intermountain Histories*, a mobile- and web-based public history app that published student-created content on western historic sites.

In 2019, following his service at the Redd Center, Cannon was named the Neil L. York Professor of History and appointed chair of the BYU history department. He served in a variety of professional associations including as president of both the Agricultural History Society and the Mormon History Association and on the editorial boards of *Agricultural History*, *BYU Studies*, and the *Utah Historical Quarterly*. In 2020, he received the Gordon Bakken Award of Merit from the Western History Association in recognition of his service to the field of western history and to the association; that service largely resulted from his ability to support western history as Redd Center director.

Selected Publications

Cannon, Brian Q., and Clyde A. Milner, II, eds. *Reconstruction and Mormon America*. Norman: University of Oklahoma Press, 2019.

Cannon, Brian Q., and Charles S. Peterson. *The Awkward State of Utah: Coming of Age in the Nation, 1896–1945*. Salt Lake City: University of Utah Press, 2015.

Embry, Jessie L., and Brian Q. Cannon, eds. *Immigrants in the Far West: Historical Identities and Experiences*. Salt Lake City: University of Utah Press, 2014.

Cannon, Brian Q. *Reopening the Frontier: Homesteading in the Modern West*. Lawrence: University Press of Kansas, 2009.

Cannon, Brian Q., and Jessie L. Embry, eds. *Utah in the Twentieth Century*. Logan: Utah State University Press, 2009.

Cannon, Brian Q. *Remaking the Agrarian Dream: New Deal Rural Resettlement in the Mountain West*. Albuquerque: University of New Mexico Press, 1996.

BRENDEN W. RENSINK

Brenden W. Rensink is the associate director of the Charles Redd Center for Western Studies and an associate professor of history at BYU. He grew up in Bellingham, Washington, and currently lives in Orem, Utah, with his wife and two children. After serving a two-year mission for The Church of Jesus Christ of Latter-day Saints in Romania and Moldova, Rensink earned a BA in history from BYU in 2003 and a MA and PhD in history from the University of Nebraska–Lincoln in 2006 and 2010. His studies focused on the North American West, Indigenous peoples, transnational borderlands, and comparative genocide studies. While a graduate student, Rensink published articles in peer-reviewed journals, including *Alternative*, *We Proceeded On*, and *Genocide Studies and Prevention*, as well as book chapters in edited collections with University of Nebraska Press, Transaction Publishers, and University of Arizona Press.

With degrees in hand, Rensink secured academic positions as an instructor at the University of Nebraska–Lincoln and Nebraska Wesleyan University in 2010 and as a visiting assistant professor at the University of Nebraska at Kearney from 2011 to 2013. In 2013, Rensink accepted a position as a historian and documentary editor with the Joseph Smith Papers project at the Church History Department in Salt Lake City, Utah. He is the coeditor of *Documents Vol. 4* and *Documents Vol. 6.*

In March 2015, Rensink accepted a new position as assistant director of the Redd Center with a concurrent position as an assistant professor of history. In 2019, BYU promoted him to the rank of associate professor and associate director. At the center, he splits time between teaching for the history department and the American Studies program, continuing his personal research projects, managing ongoing Redd Center events and programming, and starting new initiatives.

In 2015, he published a *Historical Dictionary of the American Frontier*, coauthored with Jay H. Buckley. In 2018, he published his first monograph, *Native but Foreign: Indigenous Immigrants and Refugees in the North American Borderlands*, in Texas A&M University Press's Connecting the Greater West series. The book won the 2019 Spur Award for Best Historical Nonfiction Book from the Western Writers of America. Rensink hosted an academic seminar and published the resulting scholarship as an edited anthology collection during his early days at the center. After planning and hosting the seminar with P. Jane Hafen, he and Hafen edited and published *Essays on American Indian and Mormon History* with University of Utah Press in 2019. The volume won the 2019 Metcalfe Best Anthology Book Award from the

Brenden W. Rensink

John Whitmer Historical Association. He is the editor of a brand-new anthology, *The North American West in the 21ˢᵗ Century,* published by the University of Nebraska Press in 2022. Rensink regularly presents research at academic conferences in fields of Western history, Indigenous studies, borderlands studies, and others. He is currently working on a second monograph—exploring cultural histories of wilderness experiences and adventuring in the North American West.

When searching for candidates for the associate director position, the Redd Center expressed a desire to prioritize new "digital" projects and initiatives. Rensink expanded the center's online presence by increasing social media activity and livestreaming Redd Center events. He also developed and launched the *Intermountain Histories* digital public history project in 2017. This project consists of a website and free mobile app that publish microhistories around the region. Rensink collaborates with professors from multiple universities whose students research and write "stories" and "tours," which Rensink and his student interns edit and publish. As project manager and general editor, Rensink oversees all aspects of the project's outreach, collaboration with professors, and publication. Rensink also launched the *Writing Westward* podcast in 2018 in order to provide a platform for scholars to engage with broader public audiences. This monthly podcast features conversations with authors from a variety of disciplines, academic and public, who are working on western topics. The podcast has featured a wide array of guests, from well-known, award-winning scholars to public intellectuals and amateur researchers.

Amidst these publishing and public history endeavors, the ongoing annual cycle of Redd Center activities keeps Rensink fully occupied. He is passionate about the center's mission to bridge divides between the academic and public worlds, and this perspective guides his approach to planning public programming, administering awards and sponsorships, and representing the Redd Center at various public events. The interdisciplinary vision of the center has also shaped his efforts to expand outreach to scientists, researchers, and public constituencies outside of the center's long-standing strengths in the social sciences and humanities. The Redd Center is uncommonly fortunate to have secured funding through university support and generous endowments. Rensink recognizes the rare opportunities this affords, as well as the unique responsibilities it places on the Redd Center administration to make wise use of those funds and maximize its impact for scholars and the public living in the American West.

Looking back at the diverse initiatives and broad impact the Redd Center has achieved in its first fifty years, Rensink looks forward to helping chart its next fifty, optimistic of what the center will continue to accomplish. He is likewise anxious to discover what new opportunities await the Redd Center in the years to come, as the center continues producing and supporting scholarship and engaging with the public.

Selected Publications

Rensink, Brenden W., ed. *The North American West in the 21st Century.* Lincoln: University of Nebraska Press, 2022.

Hafen, P. Jane, and Brenden W. Rensink, eds. *Essays on American Indian and Mormon History.* Salt Lake City: University of Utah Press, 2019.

Rensink, Brenden W. *Native but Foreign: Indigenous Immigrants and Refugees in the North American Borderlands.* College Station: Texas A&M University Press, 2018.

Ashurst-McGee, Mark, David Grua, Elizabeth Kuehn, and Brenden W. Rensink, eds. *The Joseph Smith Papers: Documents, Vol. 6: February 1838–August 1839.* Salt Lake City: The Church Historian's Press, 2017.

Godfrey, Matthew, and Brenden W. Rensink, eds. *The Joseph Smith Papers: Documents, Vol. 4: April 1834–October 1835.* Salt Lake City: The Church Historian's Press, 2016.

Buckley, Jay H,. and Brenden W. *Historical Dictionary of the American Frontier.* Lanham, Md.: Rowman and Littlefield, 2015.

CHAPTER 6. THE BUCKLEY YEARS, 2018–PRESENT

With Brian Q. Cannon's appointment as history department chair in August 2018, FHSS Dean Benjamin M. Ogles appointed Jay H. Buckley as director of the Charles Redd Center for Western Studies for a three-year term with the expectation of serving a minimum of two terms. Buckley, an associate professor of history specializing in western history, also directs BYU's American Indian Studies minor (AIS). Buckley's research and publication interests, his service on the Redd Center Board of Directors since 2011, and his relationship with his former student Brenden W. Rensink enabled Buckley to hit the ground running.

During his first term, Buckley built upon his predecessors' foundation while making his own contributions. Since Buckley has a joint appointment as a history professor and Redd Center director, the work of the center could not occur without the capable and talented assistance of Rensink as full-time Redd Center associate director and Amy Carlin as a part-time office specialist. With their help, the center continues to advance its outreach and contributions to western studies.[1]

One of Buckley first initiatives involved finding new ways to organize over four decades of materials at the center so that it would be easier to access and utilize. He and his staff sought out Howard Loos, the Chief Information Privacy Officer and Director of Information Management at BYU. Loos trained Buckley, Rensink, and Carlin about which records to keep hard copies of, what records can be stored digitally, and which were eligible for archival transfer.

While combing through the records, Buckley became impressed

by the many achievements and the solid foundation laid by his Redd Center predecessors—Leonard J. Arrington (1972–1980), Thomas G. Alexander (1980–1992), Jessie L. Embry (1979–2014), William A. "Bert" Wilson (1992–1996), Edward A. Geary (1996–2002), and Brian Q. Cannon (2002–2018). Buckley recognized the significant financial contributions from the Redd, Butler, Peters, Dixon, Taylor, and Embry families that had placed the center on a firm financial footing. He desired to honor these sacrifices in some fashion.

Director Buckley recognized that 2022 marked the sesquicentennial of the Redd Center's founding. He initiated a plan to commemorate the fifty years of the Redd Center's existence through a jubilee celebration on March 25, 2022. He instigated a compilation of a fifty-year administrative history to honor the legacy of the Charlie and Annaley Naegle Redd family and the history of the center.[2]

Fortunately, Buckley's dear friend Jessie L. Embry—Redd Center assistant, associate, or acting director from 1979 to 2014—provided him with a forty-page history she had compiled while working at the Redd Center. Using this as a starting point, Buckley hired undergraduate students Andra Lainhart, Camilla Richardson, Nicole (Nikki) Smith, and Emily White as research assistants. Over the course of several years, they have been indispensable in helping him research, draft, compile, and edit this volume's content.

Compiling the Redd Center's history proved valuable to Buckley in several ways. It showed him the contributions of each of the previous directors. He felt a tremendous amount of humility and gratitude to those who established the family endowments that have grown significantly and enabled the center to expand its ability to promote the study of the Intermountain West by sponsoring research, publication, teaching, and public programs in a variety of academic disciplines.

During Buckley's directorship, the center expanded the number and amounts of awards distributed through its spring competition to over $100,000 annually. As he and his students compiled a list of all the center awards given over the past five decades, Director Buckley was astounded to discover the Redd Center has awarded more than $2,002,630 to hundreds of students and faculty researching and writing about the Intermountain West.

Under his direction, the center expanded and increased its support of BYU student awards and opportunities. Buckley worked with former Associate Director Jessie Embry to sponsor four history student awards through the Bertis L. and Anna E. C. Embry Endowment. Together, they created a new Bertis L. and Anna E. C. Embry Award in Global Latter-day Saint History. The endowment also sponsors additional history student awards including the Eugene E. Campbell Award in Utah History, the Fred R. Gowans Award in 19th C. American West

Jay H. Buckley

History, and the American Indian Studies Indigenous History Award. The center also agreed to co-sponsor the William J. Snow Award in American West or Latter-day Saint History.[3]

Buckley met with Clarence Dixon Taylor family representatives John Taylor, his brother George Taylor, and cousins Ken Kartchner and Henry "Hank" Taylor to expand the number of Clarence Dixon Taylor awards given from that endowment to recognize significant publications and public programming highlighting Utah, Carbon, and Wasatch County history and economic development. The awards are open to individuals, families, communities, and institutions. Buckley worked with the family to create a new Clarence Dixon Taylor Research Grant of up to $1,500 to encourage and facilitate research about these counties in addition to continuing the existing awards for published books, articles, and exhibits.[4]

The Redd Center increased its funding amounts for four fellowships annually to K–12 teachers to enable them to attend the annual Western History Association and fellowships to K–12 teachers to attend the Western Literature Association's annual convention.[5] Buckley signed a three-year Memorandum of Understanding between the Redd Center and the Utah State Division of History to collaborate with the University of Utah and the State Historical Society in support of the Thomas G. Alexander/Miriam Murphy Editorial Fellowship at the *Utah Historical Quarterly* in recognition of Tom's contributions to the Redd Center and to Utah and western history..[6]

In 2022, Buckley and Rensink helped create the Mormon History Association's Mae Timbimboo Parry Indigenous Studies Award given to scholarly excellence in Indigenous studies presented or published in the preceding year. Submissions may include various formats of traditional scholarship such as a published book, essay, book chapter, or article. Other forms of public scholarship and engagement are also welcomed and could include public history or public programming projects, digital media, events, exhibits, advocacy, etc. The Redd Center agreed to sponsor this MHA award.

The Redd Center joined with the BYU Department of History, Africana Studies, American Indian Studies, the Anti-Human-Trafficking

Club, the BYU Black Alumni Association, and the Native American Alumni Association to seek ways to end racism in our community. Brenden Rensink chairs the BYU Slavery Project Steering Committee, which Buckley also serves on. The BYU Slavery Project involves student and faculty collaborators who study Indigenous and African American slavery connections in Utah Territory and possible benefits—direct and indirect—to the university, with recommendations on possible forms of acknowledgement and restitution.[7]

The center increased its support of BYU student scholarships and internships. Buckley signed a Memorandum of Understanding with the BYU history department to co-sponsor the Ignacio Garcia Scholarship for Indigenous and Students of Color. The Redd Center also provided new internships and opportunities for Indigenous students and students of color. During the nationwide racial unrest during the summer of 2020, Buckley issued a statement from the Redd Center opposing racism in all forms and pledging to stand together to abandon attitudes of prejudice against any of God's children to ensure *all* are afforded the same privileges of life, liberty, and the pursuit of happiness.[8]

Buckley's June 2020 letter quoted President Russell M. Nelson of The Church of Jesus Christ of Latter-day Saints, who called for humanity to repent and "abandon attitudes of prejudice against any group of God's children. . . . Any nation can only be as great as its people. That requires citizens to cultivate a moral compass that helps them distinguish between right and wrong. . . . We need to foster a fundamental respect for the human dignity of every human soul regardless of their color, creed, or cause. And we need to work tirelessly to build bridges of understanding rather than creating walls of segregation."[9]

Buckley has also expanded funding and mentoring opportunities for BYU students and faculty. The center applied for (and received) Experiential Learning Funds from the College of Family Home and Social Sciences for use in student internships and mentored research projects such as the *Intermountain Histories* digital history project, thereby promoting civic engagement, encouraging student research, and generating historical content. This work engages students in mentored scholarly projects that generate resources for the study of the

West and facilitates the hiring of Indigenous students to assist with American Indian Studies.

Because of his duties as Redd Center director, Buckley sought and received approval to name Mike Taylor (English) as an associate director of BYU's interdisciplinary AIS minor, which Buckley directs. The AIS minor found its administrative and financial home in the Redd Center in 2018. Buckley and Taylor worked together to revamp and update the curriculum, course map, website, requirements, faculty, etc. They launched an Indigenous Field Study in 2021 and created a new website: native.byu.edu. In March 2022, they conducted a Native Civil Rights Field Study, taking a dozen BYU students to Indigenous lands and places of historical significance in the Dakotas.

Occasionally, Buckley also pared down or discontinued existing center projects that no longer met desired aims. When he arrived, the Redd Center offered an interdisciplinary lecture series course on Western American Studies, American Studies 392R, taught by Rensink. Students attended research presentations by guest presenters from the life sciences, humanities, arts, and social sciences, each of whom had received research support from the Redd Center. Rensink also debuted an American Studies 301 Western American Studies seminar.[10] Nevertheless, the center continued to struggle to entice students to declare the Western American Studies minor despite considerable efforts on Rensink's part to revise and reenergize it. Buckley and Rensink jointly decided to furlough the minor in 2019. Doing so helped reallocate Rensink's time to more fruitful endeavors. The center continues influencing students through western-themed courses in the American Studies and AIS minors.

In 2019, Buckley and Rensink initiated a Redd Center summer seminar that hosted a dozen authors to workshop essays for the center's next volume. This effort resulted in an anthology edited by Brenden W. Rensink entitled *The North American West in the 21ˢᵗ Century*, slated for publication in 2022 by the University of Nebraska Press.

Looking Back, Moving Forward

The Redd Center continues to advance the study of the Intermountain West. The center continued funding promising young BYU faculty through the Mollie an Karl Butler Young Scholar Award in Western Studies.[11] The Redd Center continued funding the Lemuel Hardison Redd Jr. Professor of Western American History, an endowed chair currently held by Ignacio M. Garcia of BYU's history department (2006–present).[12] The center continued hosting visiting fellows until the COVID-19 pandemic that spread rapidly in the United States by March 2020 prevented additional visiting fellows in 2020 or Winter 2021.[13]

The Redd Center continued contributing to the study of the Intermountain West by sponsoring guest lectures and panel discussions. The center provides honoraria and travel funds for guest lecturers in western studies who visit BYU to speak to classes or deliver public lectures. Our current annual named lectures are the William A. Wilson Folklore Archives Founder's Day Lecture (co-sponsored with the William A. Wilson Folklore Archives), the Clarence Dixon Taylor Lecture, the Annaley Naegle Redd Lecture, and the William Howard and Hazel Butler Peters Lecture. These events, usually live streamed through the center's Facebook and YouTube pages, regularly have more virtual viewers than those on campus. The center also continues to host western studies faculty luncheons to promote collegiality and discussion of western studies topics.

The Redd Center continued its collaboration with the Utah Humanities Council, the Utah State Historical Society, and the University of Utah in sponsoring conferences and lectures elsewhere throughout Utah. We sponsored prizes and events in conjunction with professional organizations including the Western History Association, the Western Literature Association, the Western Political Science Association, Phi Alpha Theta, the Western Museum Association, the Native American Literature Symposium, the Mormon History Association, the Utah State Historical Society, and the Buffalo Bill Historical Association. The center supported National History Day competitions in the affiliated states of the Intermountain West.

Meanwhile, Brenden W. Rensink received a promotion from assistant to associate professor in the history department and a similar promotion to associate director of the Redd Center in 2019. He earned a well-deserved sabbatical for fall 2021.[14] As the only full-time center employee, Rensink oversees many of the center's sponsored lectures, public history projects, and public programming. He and Carlin ably manage the center's awards programs, publicity, and media. Rensink also produces a semiannual newsletter that notifies thousands of subscribers of Redd Center activities and manages the center's social media accounts, *Intermountain Histories*, *Writing Westward*, and the BYU Slavery Project on Facebook and Twitter.

A few months before Buckley took over as director, Rensink initiated the *Intermountain Histories* digital public project. Faculty and students from seven universities have participated in the project as collaborators, including several from BYU. Beginning in 2018, Rensink launched an internship program wherein one to three interns study public history, conduct research, and publish stories of their own. More than three hundred undergraduate and graduate students have contributed. During 2020 Rensink edited and published approximately one hundred additional stories researched and written by student contributors, bringing the total to nearly 450 stories published.[15]

With Director Buckley's approbation, Rensink launched a second public history venture in 2018 with a Redd Center podcast entitled *Writing Westward*, for which Rensink hosts interviews with western authors. This project allows the center to engage with more scholars, gives them a platform to discuss their work, and engages the public through new mediums. Rensink acts as host, producer, sound engineer, publicity manager, and every other role of this complex endeavor, yet he has been able to produce roughly one new episode per month with diverse guests and topics.[16]

Other recent changes at the center included creating a new Redd Center logo, Carlin and Rensink updated and modernized the center's website and application portal, and Buckley and Rensink received new furniture and shelving for outdated models in their 954 Spencer W. Kimball Tower offices. BYU's Charles Redd Center for Western Studies is excited to see what the next fifty years will bring with regards to the study of the Intermountain West and looks forward to actively helping that scholarship come to pass.

1 In 2020, the Redd Center unveiled a new logo for use on social media platforms and published an updated brochure.

2 Buckley solicited the help of Jessie L. Embry, who graciously shared her knowledge and historical writing skills to provide initial drafts of many of the chapters. BYU undergraduate students Camilla Richardson, Emily White, and Andra Lainhart proved indispensable in researching, drafting, compiling, and editing portions of the history. Redd Center office specialist Amy Carlin masterfully completed the editing and layout for this jubilee publication.

3 We are grateful to Jessie L. Embry for her support of these endeavors in honor of her parents.

4 These awards and grants are named for a representative of the Dixon and Taylor families who established an endowment in memory of these families' contribution to the economic development of Provo and central Utah. Recipients of the Clarence Dixon Taylor awards can be found in Appendix 5.

5 The Redd Center continued to reach out to professional organizations to support research in western studies. The center awards the Best Paper on the Politics of the American West at the Western Political Science Association, the Beatrice Medicine Awards in American Indian Studies at the Native American Literature Symposium, and the Western Museum Association Award for Exhibition Excellence. They fund the Arrington–Prucha Prize for the best article of the year in Western American Religious History as well as the Jensen–Miller Award for the best article in the field of women and gender in the North American West at the Western History Association. Additional awards are distributed to the Pacific Coast Branch of the American Historical Association and the Rural American West Paper Competition, awarded by the AAG Rural Geography Specialty Group. The center awards a Phi Alpha Theta Book Award for the best book in western American history.

6 The center continued awarding the best general interest article of the year appearing in the *Utah Historical Quarterly*. For example, see Larry R. Gerlach, "Appropriation and Accommodation: The University of Utah and the Utes," *Utah Historical Quarterly* 85, no. 3 (Summer 2017): 204–223.

7 This project joins a growing community of universities studying the impact and legacies of slavery in their campus histories. For more information, see byuslaveryproject.org.

8 One initial response has been to study ways the Redd Center and our sponsoring institution have benefitted directly or indirectly from Indigenous and African slavery or servitude in Utah Territory pre-1863. Charlie Redd's great grandparents John H. and Elizabeth Redd sold their land

in Murfreesboro, Tennessee, freed their slaves, and immigrated to Utah Territory. Two African American women, Venus and Chaney, and their four children, continued to live with the Redds. Redd, *The Utah Redds and Their Progenitors*, 197. See also, Tonya Reiter, "Redd Slave Histories: Family, Race, and Sex in Pioneer Utah," *Utah Historical Quarterly* 85 no. 2 (Spring 2017): 109–26.

9 President Russell M. Nelson, "We Are All Children of God." June 1, 2020.

10 Faculty in the history department typically teach five courses a year. Buckley receives a course release during winter and fall semesters due to director responsibilities at the Redd Center.

11 See Appendix 4.

12 Professor Ignacio M. García, a pioneer in Mexican American Studies, is a prolific historian of Latino Studies. His work illuminates the emergence of Latinos as a major political and cultural force in the region. For a list of previous endowed chair holders, see Appendix 3a.

13 The last three visiting fellows were Vanja Polić Jurkovic (associate professor of English at University of Zagreb) in 2018, Michael G. Boyden (associate professor of American Literature at Uppsala University, Sweden) in 2019, and Paul Formisano (associate professor of English at the University of South Dakota) in 2020.

14 Rensink's monograph, *Native but Foreign: Indigenous Immigrants and Refugees in the North American Borderlands* (College Station: Texas A&M University Press, 2018), won the 2019 Spur Award for Best Historical Nonfiction Book. His co-edited anthology, *Essays on American Indian and Mormon History* (Salt Lake City: University of Utah Press, 2019), won the 2019 Metcalfe Best Anthology Book Award from the John Whitmer Historical Association. Rensink was named the Marjorie Pay Hinckley Young Scholar for the FHSS College at BYU for 2020–2023 and received a well-deserved sabbatical.

15 Site analytics recorded an average of 3,500–5,250 users and 5,500–7,500 page views per month in 2020.

16 All episodes are available at writingwestward.org and via Apple Podcasts, Spotify, Stitcher, and various other podcast apps and distribution networks.

JAY H. BUCKLEY

Jay Harry Buckley was born in Evanston, Wyoming, to Jack H and Carol Joy (Wirig) Buckley on November 3, 1969. The youngest of six children, Buckley grew up on a cattle and sheep ranch in Lyman, Wyoming. His family also owned another ranch straddling the Utah–Wyoming border along the north slope of the Uinta Mountains near Lonetree, Wyoming. The original homesteader, George Bullock, was good friends with Butch Cassidy, who often stayed at the ranch.

Beaver Creek of Henry's Fork (Green River) flows through the Buckley Lonetree ranch only a dozen miles from the first Rocky Mountain fur trade rendezvous site in 1825. Meanwhile, the Buckley Bridger Valley ranch lies just a few miles downstream from the Fort Bridger State Historic Site. Both ranch locations inspired Jay's interest in the American West, American Indians, and the mountain man and rendezvous era.

Buckley began attending BYU in 1988. He served a mission for The Church of Jesus Christ of Latter-day Saints in the South Africa Cape Town Mission from 1989 to 1991, during South African President F.W. de Klerk's ending of South Africa's apartheid policies. Buckley was living among and teaching the restored gospel to Nelson Mandela's Xhosa-speaking Thembu Nation in Umtata (Mthatha) when President de Klerk released Mandela from prison on February 11, 1990. Both de Klerk and his subsequent successor, Mandela, received the Nobel Peace Prize in 1993.

Upon completing his mission, Buckley returned to BYU in 1991,

and two significant events hap-
pened. First, he met Rebecca "Becky"
Daynes, and they were married in
the Salt Lake Temple in 1992. They
are the parents of three children, David, Mary, and Jared. Second, Buckley enrolled in two history courses
taught by Professor Fred R. Gowans
covering the American West and
American Indians. After taking these
courses, Buckley declared history as
his major and graduated with a BA in
history in 1994. With Gowans as his

Buckley receiving an award from Mark Weekley, Superintendent of the Lewis and Clark National Historic Trail, NPS

mentor, Buckley wrote his master's thesis on mountain man Robert
Campbell and received his MA in history from BYU in 1996.

Buckley enrolled in a history PhD program at the University of
Nebraska–Lincoln and studied with renowned Lewis and Clark expert
Gary E. Moulton, editor of *The Journals of Lewis and Clark Expedi-
tion*. Working as a research assistant to John R. Wunder, director of the
Center for Great Plains Studies, Buckley completed his coursework at
the Lincoln campus. The University of Nebraska–Lincoln and Nebras-
ka Wesleyan University both hired him as an adjunct history instruc-
tor while he completed his dissertation on Superintendent of Indian
Affairs William Clark, which won the Lewis E. Atherton Dissertation
Prize from the State Historical Society of Missouri in 2001.

Upon his graduation in 2001, BYU's history department hired Buckley in the fall semester of 2001 to replace the retiring Gowans. Buckley
returned to Provo, Utah, in the fall of 2001 and began teaching courses in American West, American Indian, and US history. He revised his
award-winning dissertation into *William Clark: Indian Diplomat* (2008),
which received the Missouri History Book Award for best Missouri biography from the State Historical Society of Missouri and the Eagleton–
Waters Book Award for the best book on Missouri political history. BYU
promoted him to associate professor of history in 2008.

The Lewis and Clark National Historic Trail Interpretive Center and the Portage Route Chapter of the Lewis and Clark Trail Heritage Foundation selected Buckley as a Scholar-in-Residence at Great Falls, Montana, in 2004 during the Lewis and Clark Bicentennial. The national Lewis and Clark Trail Heritage Foundation awarded Buckley a Meritorious Achievement Award for his Lewis and Clark scholarship in 2010. The membership of the Lewis and Clark Trail Heritage Foundation elected Buckley to their board of directors in 2006 and Buckley served as national president from 2011 to 2012. The foundation provides leadership on scholarship, education, and conservation pertaining to the Lewis and Clark National Historic Trail. Lewis and Clark National Historic Trail Superintendent Mark Weekley presented Buckley with the National Park Service's distinguished merit medallion for his exemplary service in 2012. In 2018, Buckley delivered the inaugural Gary E. Moulton Lecture at the Lewis and Clark National Historic Trail headquarters in Omaha, Nebraska. He continues to serve on the editorial board of the peer-reviewed journal *We Proceeded On*.

Buckley directs college-credit field studies every summer for the Driven2Teach Program (driven2teach.org), which offers Utah educators grades 4–12 who specialize in American History a hands-on learning experience at historical sites around the country. History department chair Don Harreld selected Buckley to receive the Outstanding Teacher Award in 2015. He has been a visiting scholar for the Gilder Lehrman Institute of American History since 2018. Buckley has also served on the Orem Historic Preservation Commission for more than a decade. In addition to teaching history courses, Buckley has also directed the American Indian Studies minor at BYU since 2001.

BYU's Redd Center selected Buckley as their Mollie and Karl Butler Young Scholar in Western Studies (2006–08). Redd Center Director Brian Q. Cannon invited Buckley to join the Redd Center board of directors in 2012. Benjamin M. Ogles, dean of the College of Family, Home, and Social Sciences, appointed Buckley director of the Redd Center in 2018, replacing Cannon, who had accepted a new position as history department chair. Buckley's first term as Redd Center director began September 1, 2018.

Selected Publications

Woods, Fred E., Jay H. Buckley, and Hunter Hallows, eds. *The Life and Adventures of Mr. Eli Wiggill: South African 1820 Settler, Wesleyan Missionary, and Latter-day Saint.* Draper, UT: Greg Kofford Books, 2022. [in press]

Buckley, Jay H. *The Charles Redd Center for Western Studies at Brigham Young University: A Golden Jubilee History, 1972–2022.* Provo, UT: Charles Redd Center for Western Studies, 2022.

Chaves, Kelly K., and Oliver C. Walton, with Jay H. Buckley, and Jeffery D. Nokes. *Explorers of the American East: Mapping the World through Primary Documents.* Santa Barbara, CA: ABC-CLIO, 2018.

Buckley, Jay H., and Jeffery D. Nokes. *Explorers of the American West: Mapping the World through Primary Documents.* Santa Barbara, CA: ABC-CLIO, 2016.

Buckley, Jay H., and Brenden W. Rensink. *Historical Dictionary of the American Frontier.* Lanham, MD: Rowman & Littlefield, 2015.

Harris, Matthew L., and Jay H. Buckley, eds. *Zebulon Pike, Thomas Jefferson, and the Opening of the American West.* Norman: University of Oklahoma Press, 2012.

Buckley, Jay H., Chase Arnold, Orem Public Library. *Orem [Utah].* Charleston: Arcadia Publishing, 2010.

Buckley, Jay H. *William Clark: Indian Diplomat.* Norman: University of Oklahoma Press, 2008.

Buckley, Jay H., John D. W. Guice, and James J. Holmberg. *By His Own Hand? The Mysterious Death of Meriwether Lewis.* Norman: University of Oklahoma Press, 2006.

CHAPTER 7. FAMILY ENDOWMENTS

Lemuel H. Redd Jr. Endowment

Biographies of Charles "Charlie" and Annaley Naegle Redd and ancestors

Charlie Redd

Annaley Naegle Redd

Charles and Annaley Redd Foundation

Lemuel Hardison Redd Jr., Eliza Westover, Lucy Zina Lyman

Lemuel Hardison Redd Sr., Keziah Jane Butler, Sarah Louisa Chamberlain

John Hardison Redd and Elizabeth Hancock

John Topham and Susan Redd Butler Endowment

John Topham and Susan Redd Butler Endowment

Biographies of the Butler and Peters families and ancestors

John Lowe and Caroline Skeen Butler I

John Lowe and Nancy Smith Butler II

John Topham and Susan Redd Butler

Karl and Mollie Parker Butler

William Howard and Hazel Butler Peters

Bertis and Anna Embry Endowment

Biographies of the Embry family

Clarence Dixon Taylor Endowment

Biographies of the Dixon and Taylor Families

CHARLIE REDD

Charles "Charlie" Redd was the sixth of eight children born to Lemuel Hardison "Lem" Redd Jr. and Eliza Ann Westover on May 8, 1889, in Bluff, Utah. It was a difficult birth in a small, three-room log cabin with a dirt roof and a dirt floor. His parents quickly gave him a name and a blessing in case he did not survive long. But against all odds, Charlie did survive. The Redd family tradition of raising livestock started with Charlie's grandfather Lemuel Hardison Redd Sr., director of the Kanara Cattle and Sheep Company in New Harmony, Utah, and has continued for generations. At the age of six, Charlie began helping his father tend the L. H. Redd Company sheep herds.[1]

Charlie's childhood was influenced by the diverse settlers from different European nations. He employed and worked alongside Hispanic Americans, Anglos, and Native peoples. These relationships taught him about different languages, cultures, and traditions. After contracting pleurisy at age eleven, Charlie developed a heart issue that required an operation in Salt Lake City. During this time, he forged a special bond with his mother. This health setback affected his mission assignment for The Church of Jesus Christ of Latter-day Saints and his eligibility for the draft during World War I.

In 1908, Charlie moved to Provo, Utah, to study agriculture and business at Brigham Young High School (BY High). BY High began as Brigham Young Academy (BYA) in 1876 as a secondary school that grew to include grades K–12. In 1903, BYA had been dissolved and replaced by BY High and Brigham Young University. Peers and teachers at BY High described Charlie as "bright and eager to learn." Charlie was very popular with his classmates and was frequently mentioned in the school newspaper for sports, politics, and debate. Baseball was the school's favorite sport at that time, and Charlie played catcher and worked as team manager. He also starred on the basketball team.

Charlie Redd, ca. 1913

During his senior year, he served as the class president.[2] His class yearbook for 1911 described him as follows: "Charles Redd, born Bluff, Utah; resided La Sal and Provo, Utah. Agriculture and High School. Charles was raised among the lofty mountains of San Juan and was early inspired with high ideals. He has been our class president and has

Charlie Redd, left, as BYU baseball catcher with pitcher Don Johnson, right

represented us in every phase of school life. Member of Student Body Executive Committee. A leader and a pusher."[3]

After completing his studies, Charlie received a mission call for The Church of Jesus Christ of Latter-day Saints in 1911. Charlie's original call was to the Southern States Mission, but he was reassigned to the Pacific Northwest Mission (1911–1913) because of his childhood surgery. Charlie served most of his mission in Washington state. Missionaries typically spent fall, winter, and spring proselyting in town and taught in the surrounding rural areas during the summer. During his mission, Charlie transferred to the mission home in Portland, Oregon, and served as a branch president and mission secretary to President Melvin J. Ballard. After two and a half years of missionary service, Charlie returned home to southeastern Utah.

In 1914, Lem Redd and others purchased the Cunningham and Carpenter and Sommerville Brothers livestock operations at La Sal, Utah, which they renamed the La Sal Livestock Company. They installed Charlie as manager on January 1, 1915. He moved to La Sal to fulfill his duties and eventually purchased the company outright from the other shareholders. Over a period of fifty years, Charlie purchased numerous ranches in Utah and Colorado to expand their holdings from Utah's La Sal Mountains in the north to the Navajo Reservation in the south, and from Telluride in the east to the Colorado River in Utah's Canyonlands to the west.[4] Colorado ranch properties included Summer Camp, Harmon Place, Goat Creek, Akin Place, Plateau, Herndon Ranch, Gurley Lake, Groundhog Lake, Belmear Lake, Fitch Place, and Desert Claim and held six forest service grazing permits. Altogether, these ranches held a carrying capacity of approximately one thousand mother cows and twenty thousand ewe sheep. Redd Ranches headquarters remained at La Sal.[5]

Charlie oversaw all ranching activities: he hired employees; managed farming operations; supervised the sheep flocks and cattle herds; built fences, corrals, and buildings; hauled salt; and baled hay. Through hard work, frugality, and wise investments, he gradually expanded and improved ranching operations. Charlie willingly took calculated risks—an experimental turkey operation did not last long, but a dairy operation lasted for years. He created almost a company town at La Sal that included a store, a gas station, and a post office, and Charlie himself served as postmaster for fifty years. He also operated a Chevrolet and farm machinery dealership.[6] He often wore a frayed Pendleton jacket and patched overalls and liked to drive Chevys.[7]

Charlie learned of a sheep and wool improvement program at New Mexico State University, which inspired him to work on increasing the productivity and of his sheep flock. He learned important lessons that allowed him to become a leader in the livestock industry, both locally and nationally. This research required Charlie and his employees to pay close attention to the different characteristics of the sheep. For example, they rated the quality of the wool and kept those sheep with better quality wool as breeding stock and culled those with poorer quality wool, sending them to slaughter. Charlie worked with family members and other employees to improve his sheep business. In the 1960s, he sent his son Paul to study the sheep industry in Australia to apply useful improvements to their sheep herds.

Charlie also focused on improving his cattle through breeding and enhancing the grazing range in this high elevation environment. Charlie understood the challenge of managing a ranch and the test it presented to both brain and brawn. He improved the carrying capacity of some of his range tenfold through brush eradication and grass planting. "The real joy," Charlie insisted, "the ultimate satisfaction of land ownership, is to see the land and the livestock improve under one's own hand. When any natural resource becomes more fruitful, more beautiful through your own personal efforts, there is a real sense of partnership with the Creator."[8]

As manager, Charlie raised chickens and pigs and cultivated a large garden to meet the culinary needs of employees. He planted crested wheat grass on the rangelands managed by the federal government and grew alfalfa and grain for the livestock.[9] Notably, Charlie received the 1946 "Man of the Year in Livestock" award from the *Record Stockman* weekly magazine. His son Hardy said, "the best manager for a piece of land is the footprint of the owner."[10]

Being a good conservationist meant being a good steward of the land and water. Charlie studied the attributes manifested by the hardiest cattle that could survive and thrive in the desert high country. Then he purchased bulls that provided those necessary characteristics to the next generation. Over time, he started selling gain-rated performance bulls to individual ranchers throughout the Intermountain West. Later, the Redds began holding an annual bull sale auction on the first Saturday in May. Buyers examined the animals and their records, enjoyed a beef-and-beans lunch, and purchased bulls.[11]

Charlie had a short-lived marriage (1921–25) to Ethel Moore, a woman from Moab. The love of his life, however, was Annaley Naegle. They first met when her mother and siblings came to La Sal, where her grandparents worked for Charlie. When Annaley and her sister Pearl lived in Provo, Charlie occasionally visited them and took them out to dinner. After Annaley graduated with her teaching credentials, she returned to La Sal to teach at the local one-room school. She also worked part time at the store and as Charlie's secretary, and their love blossomed. Charlie said his best and happiest day was when he mar-

La Sal Live Stock and Store, ca. 1950: the "center place" of La Sal Livestock Company and Redd Ranches

ried Annaley on August 29, 1931. When asked why she married a man twenty-one years older than herself, Annaley responded, "Charlie needed me!" The couple had nine children, eight of whom survived to adulthood, and spent forty-four happy years together.

Charlie Redd, ca. 1930

Charlie dealt with the uncertainties of drought and financial depression during the 1920s and 1930s. Banks trusted him, however, and he was able to keep the ranch operational during the Great Depression. At one time, bankers showed up to count the sheep to verify his loan's security. In response, Charlie convinced the bankers of the reality of their collateral by bringing twenty-five thousand sheep to the roadside. Equally important, the bankers stayed at the ranch house and ate with the family and employees. Recognizing that the ranch was self-sufficient, the bankers agreed to finance the ranch for another year. Family lore declares that Annaley's delicious beans helped save the ranch.[12]

Charlie's diverse career was not limited to ranching; he also held multiple positions around La Sal. He served as president of the State Bank of San Juan until the Great Depression forced a merger. He also served as director of the Federal Land Bank, the Blanding Irrigation Company, the Grayson Cooperative Store, Utah Power and Light, the Amalgamated Sugar Company, and Pacific National Life Assurance Company. He was an organizer and president of the National Wool Marketing Association, president of the first local Bureau of Land Management advisory board, and chair of the Utah Water and Power Board. He served on the Utah State University board of trustees and on a regional executive committee of the Boy Scouts of America.[13]

Charlie avidly studied politics, and his children remember listening from the stairs to their father's political discussions with guests when the children were supposed to be in bed. Charlie served in the Utah State Legislature from 1924 to 1930, and he served three times as a delegate to the Republican National Convention. Some asked him to run for governor of Utah, but he declined. His most successful legislation was the Redd Act, which allowed for betting in horse races. He later sponsored its repeal due to what he saw as corruption. Charlie retired from the legislature after serving for six years.[14]

The Redds hosted foreign dignitaries at the ranch, including Lord and Lady Halifax. Lord Halifax had served as the British Foreign Minister prior to World War II, before serving as ambassador to the United States. He frequently traveled throughout the US to thank the American people for their support of the war. He and his staff came to La

Sal once after WWII. Other British officials and dignitaries also stayed with the Redds, and when Queen Elizabeth II came to the United States in 1957, Charlie was one of five Americans selected to receive the Order of the British Empire for "outstanding service in the cause of Anglo-American friendship and understanding." Charlie, Annaley, and their oldest daughter Kathy accepted the invitation to attend the ceremony at the British Embassy.[15]

Charlie was as much at home with the Queen of England as he was with everyone else. He associated with Church leaders, university professors, and government officials. Yet he was also comfortable with ranch foreman, store clerks, cowboys, and sheep herders. Many felt that he was a demanding employer, but they acknowledged he treated employees fairly and honestly.

Charlie had a special bond of love with his children. According to Arrington, "Although there might have been some distance and objectivity to his experience, he probably enjoyed them more than he would have done if he had been younger."[16] Charlie particularly enjoyed traveling with the children, and they have fond memories of special trips. However, it was frustrating for the children when Charlie sometimes forgot he had brought them along and inadvertently left them behind, though he always returned to bring them home.

Charlie and Annaley expressed concerns for their children's education in the schoolhouse, so they sent the oldest two, Kathy and Hardy, to Wasatch Academy in Mount Pleasant, Utah. Feeling that boarding school was not an ideal situation, the Redds built a lovely home in Provo, where the children could attend Brigham Young Elementary and BY High. Each of Charlie and Annaley Redd's children—Katheryn Anne, Charles Hardison, Robert Byron, Paul David, Maraley, Beverly, Regina, and Rebecca Sue—graduated from BY High.

Charlie Redd suffered a stroke in April 1969. His mind remained alert, but he spent the rest of his life unable to speak or drive. Annaley cared for him until his death in Provo on March 30, 1975. Three years before his passing, the Redd family established the Charles Redd Center for Western Studies in 1972 and the Lemuel H. Redd Jr. Chair in Western History. Charlie stated: "I would like somehow to get into the hearts and souls of young people the lessons of history, particularly those of Western America. The American pioneer has much to teach us. . . . Learning of the successful settlement of this country, we may gain courage to face squarely the challenges and problems of present-day frontiers."[17] Charlie and Annaley Redd's family legacy lives on through the Charles Redd Center for Western Studies. Its mission promotes the study of the Intermountain West region the Redd family loved so much.

Charlie Redd and Queen Elizabeth II

Charlie Redd in later years

1 Leonard J. Arrington, *Charlie Redd: Utah's Audacious Stockman* (Logan: Utah State University Press, 1995), 37.

2 Arrington, *Charlie Redd: Utah's Audacious Stockman*, 48, 55.

3 BYHS Yearbook, 1911.

4 Roger Neville Williams, "Giants of the Far Country: Five Generations of Ranching the Rockies," *Rocky Mountain Magazine* (September/October 1981), 34–38.

5 Redd Ranches of Colorado brochure, Charles Redd Center for Western Studies.

6 Karl E. Young, "Charles Redd: Profile of a Renaissance Man as Rancher," in *Charles Redd Monographs in Western History* no. 5, *Essays on the American West, 1973-1974*, Thomas G. Alexander, ed. (Provo: Brigham Young University Press, 1975): 106–31.

7 Williams, "Giants of the Far Country," 36.

8 Redd Ranches brochure, Charles Redd Center for Western Studies.

9 Arrington, *Charlie Redd: Utah's Audacious Stockman*, 95; Jessie L. Embry, "Redd Ranches," Redd Ranches Collection, Harold B. Lee Library, 2007.

10 Hardy Redd, personal interview, February 6, 2022.

11 Arrington, *Charlie Redd: Utah's Audacious Stockman*, 95; Jessie L. Embry, "Redd Ranches," Redd Ranches Collection, Harold B. Lee Library, 2007.

12 Annaley Redd, "American Western Ranching: Reminiscences of My Life on a Ranch," talk given at Brigham Young University, September 1989.

13 Young, "Charles Redd: Profile of a Renaissance Man as Rancher," 106–31.

14 Young, "Charles Redd: Profile of a Renaissance Man as Rancher," 106–31.

15 Arrington, *Charlie Redd: Utah's Audacious Stockman*, 166.

16 Arrington, *Charlie Redd: Utah's Audacious Stockman*, 185.

17 Charlie Redd, quote found in the Charles Redd Center for Western Studies biographical description collection.

ANNALEY NAEGLE REDD

Annaley Naegle was born August 27, 1910, in Colonia Morelos, Sonora, Mexico, to Millicent Dorothy Jameson and John Conrad Naegle Jr. Annaley's mother was Naegle's second plural wife. The Naegles had prospered in Mexico, but Annaley never knew that life. When she was two years old, Pancho Villa forced Latter-day Saint families to flee the Mormon colonies during the Mexican Revolution. Her father believed he could not cohabit with both wives in the United States, so her mother and four children moved in with Annaley's maternal grandparents, Alexander and Amelia Jameson, in Castle Dale, Utah. Later, the two Naegle families lived in the same town, but Annaley had minimal contact with her father. Annaley grew close to her sisters, Iva and Pearl, and her brother, Keppler. When Annaley was twelve, her mother decided to move to Ammon, Idaho, where members of her family had settled. On the way north, they stopped in La Sal, where Annaley's maternal grandparents had moved to dry farm and work for Charlie Redd. The La Sal Livestock Company hired Annaley's mother Millicent as a cook. The Naegles settled in the area for a year while the children attended the local school before moving on to Ammon.

Like most youth in the area, Annaley and her siblings worked in the fields, thinning sugar beets and harvesting potatoes. At Ammon High School, Annaley enjoyed literature classes and played forward on the basketball team for coach D.T. Williams. Her brother, Keppler, was the star on the men's basketball team. Annaley loved music and sang in the Glee Club. She won an oratory contest with a speech entitled

"Which Way, America." One of Annaley's favorite teachers was Miss Ione Harris, who oversaw English and physical education and directed school plays. Annaley enjoyed theater and participated all four years. She was cast as Hazel Robinson in the senior production of *Apple Sauce.* She served as class officer her senior year when Ammon High boasted seventy-eight students comprising all four years. She excelled

Annaley (right) with her sister, Iva "Auntie Pat" Balmer (left), ca. 1932 at the La Sal ranch house

at writing and provided school publications with activity reporting. Moreover, she received excellent grades and was a member of the "A" Club. She graduated from Ammon High School on May 15, 1928.[1]

After graduation, Annaley and her sister Pearl moved to Provo, where they attended school, Annaley at the BYU Normal Training School for teacher education and Pearl at BY High. While there, Charlie Redd often visited and took the Naegle girls and their roommates to dinner. After completing her teaching certificate degree, Annaley accepted a job to teach in the two-room schoolhouse in La Sal, and she and Pearl lived near the school. The sisters felt at home and accepted in the community. Besides teaching, Annaley worked in the store and as Charlie's secretary. When the school year was over, she returned to Idaho. Redd followed her and invited her to a family reunion. While Naegle said that they never really courted, she adored Charlie and would do anything for him. They continued to see each other and married on August 29, 1931, in Farmington, Utah. Annaley was twenty-one, and Charlie was forty-two. The couple was sealed together for time and all eternity, along with their children, in the Salt Lake Temple in 1951. They had nine children—Katheryn Anne "Kathy" (Gary Mullins), Charles Hardison "Hardy" (Sonya "Sunny"), Annaley (died in infancy), Robert Byron (Mary), Paul David (Diane), Maraley (Richard Rasmussen), Beverly (Loyd Woods), Regina (James Mitchell), and Rebecca Sue "Becky" (Brian Lambert).

After the wedding, Annaley and Charlie were en route to Yellowstone for a honeymoon when he received word that the San Juan Bank was failing and needed to close. Rather than continuing the trip, the couple returned home. Charlie invited the shareholders to a dinner where he explained the situation. Annaley remembered that despite the bad news, the shareholders left in good spirits. She provided a loyal and essential partner to Charlie, an anchor through all the ups and downs of ranching, parenting, political and economic upheaval, health challenges, and life in general. She always supported Charlie in his business ventures. She typed his letters, cooked the meals for the ranch hands when there was not a cook, planned socials, and raised the children. During an IRS hearing, the government prosecutor badgered her on the stand, belittling her role as a legitimate partner. The attorney said "You don't round up cattle. You don't brand calves. Just what do you do if you're a partner in a ranch?" Annaley replied, "I produce partners!"[2]

Charlie showed his appreciation and love by taking Annaley on trips, including annual excursions to see Broadway productions in New York City. Once, she was asked to model some clothes at the Western Livestock Show. Charlie encouraged her to do it and then surprised her with the clothes at Christmas. Typical of American homes at the time, there was a division of work between men and women. Charlie told Annaley he would take care of the boys, while she was in charge of the daughters. Her support and acumen contributed to Charlie's accomplishments. When Charlie modestly suggested he did not know why Queen Elizabeth II honored him with the Most Excellent Order of the British Empire, Annaley, who had entertained the British guests, responded, "If he didn't deserve it, I did."[3]

Annaley not only supported the ranch; she also learned the business. In a 1989 lecture she gave at BYU as an honored graduate at homecoming, she explained, "The most important traits in beef cattle are highly heritable, so we began using arithmetic rather than opinion as a major tool for selecting breeding stock. We weighed the cattle and kept production records. We bought a half interest in a bull named Brae Arden 5012, whose calves had a record of faster growth on less feed than any calves on record. Performance testing became the rule at Redd Ranches. Charlie was sold on it. He preached it constantly to anyone who would listen."[4]

As the children grew, Charlie and Annaley were concerned about the children's education. For that reason, they sent the two oldest, Kathy and Hardy, to Wasatch Academy in Mount Pleasant, Utah. However, Charlie and Annaley felt boarding school was not the answer, so they moved to Provo and built a home in the "Tree Streets" neighborhood. All the children graduated from BY High, and the younger ones also attended Brigham Young Elementary until it was discontinued. The family typically split their time between La Sal and Provo so the children could access Provo's improved educational opportunities and Charlie could oversee ranch operations. During the summer, the children returned to La Sal, where the boys were in sheep or cow camps. The girls helped Annaley at the cabin, where they baked bread and made butter and cheese.

Wherever they were living, Charlie often brought guests to their home, and Annaley graciously fed them. The family held Christmas parties for employees and neighbors in La Sal. Charlie continued that tradition in Provo, inviting their neighbors. The children went to the local Latter-day Saint ward and participated in activities that their par-

Annaley, Kathy, and Charlie at the Queen's ball in New York, 1957

ents also occasionally attended. Charlie and Annaley supported and sent their sons on missions. Charlie was often away on business, but Annaley enjoyed the quiet time at home. When he was home, they both participated in neighborhood activities, including a book club.

The Redd family on the stairs at 1111 Aspen Avenue, Provo, Utah, ca. 1958
Front to back: Annaley, Charlie, Becky, Hardy, Paul, Kathy, Gina, Robert, Maraley, and Bev

All of that changed when Charlie suffered a stroke in April 1969. For the next six years, Annaley cared for him: she read to him and met his every need. Charlie had already agreed to fund a western studies center before his stroke. When the Charles Redd Center for Western Studies was established in 1972, Annaley and Hardy worked out the final arrangements for donating the money and their beloved Provo home at 1111 Aspen Avenue to the university. The Redds purchased a condominium in Three Fountains where Annaley could attend to Charlie. Although he could not talk, his mind remained sharp, and this sometimes led to miscommunication. Their daughter Beverly remembered trying to figure out what her father wanted when he felt he needed a haircut. Annaley said that Charlie often tried to grab the steering wheel when he wanted to go somewhere. She continued to care for him until his death on March 30, 1975.

Following Charlie's death, Annaley divided her time between homes in Provo and La Sal. She purchased the recently restored Naegle family winery home in Tocqueville, Utah. She continued to attend the Redd Ranches Bull Sale, help with the lunch, and attend Redd Center activities. The center named the Annaley Naegle Redd Assistantship Awards after her due to her passionate interest in the heritage of the West and invited her to lunch with the annual winners, which continued the social contact she craved. She was an avid BYU sports fan and especially enjoyed following the football team.

Annaley was supportive of the center and its activities. When she spoke at BYU in 1989, she recalled, "Our family is very proud of the Redd Center for Western Studies and the good efforts of Tom Alexander and his crew." The center advertised the new assistantships named in her honor, as well as new student research awards. When the Redd Center staff attended Paul's bull sale in Paradox, Annaley would say, "Now we can have a bull sale. The Redd Center is here." The Redd Center reciprocated the feeling when she came to the annual banquet: "Now we can have a dinner. Annaley is here." She always wore a red dress to these functions to show her support for the family and the center. She was a kind, gracious woman who always went out of her way to support the center's activities.

The family gathered when Annaley passed away on August 19, 2000. At the time, she had forty-one grandchildren and fifty-seven great-grandchildren. Her family wrote in her obituary, Annaley "created an orderly and welcoming home, serving up marvelous meals, perfect hot cakes, chicken noodle soup, prairie fire beans, and the best bread in the world. Her hands beautified her yard and garden. Annaley loved all things beautiful: flowers, music, and sunsets. She got satisfaction from a job well done. She lived a joy-filled life."[5] A famous Mark Twain quote applies to all those who knew and loved Annaley, especially Charlie: "Wheresoever she was, there was Eden."[6]

Annaley (left) with sisters Pearl and Iva, ca. 1990

1   *Ammon High School Yearbook*, Ammon, Idaho, Annaley Naegle, Class of 1928. *The Gleam*, published by the Student Body of the Ammon High School, 1928. Both items in the Redd family private collection.

2   Roger Neville Williams, "Giants of the Far Country: Five Generations of Ranching the Rockies," *Rocky Mountain Magazine* (September/October 1981), 34–38.

3   Leonard J. Arrington, *Charlie Redd: Utah's Audacious Stockman* (Logan: Utah State University Press, 1995), 168.

4   Annaley Naegle Redd, "American Western Ranching: Reminiscences of My Life on a Ranch," speech given at Brigham Young University, September 1989, copy in the Charles Redd Center for Western Studies.

5   Annaley Naegle Redd obituary, *Deseret News*, August 21, 2000.

6   Mark Twain, *The Diaries of Adam and Eve* (London: Hesperus Press, 2002).

CHARLES AND ANNALEY NAEGLE REDD FOUNDATION

Charlie and Annaley Naegle Redd left a legacy of generosity, and they taught this behavior to their children. They also encouraged their children to continue to meet and support each other. To that end, Charlie and Annaley created the Charles and Annaley Redd Foundation and set aside funds the children could distribute at an annual meeting. The foundation has funded programs and activities related to San Juan County and family interests. It continues to provide funds for Redd Center programs, including annual contributions to Redd Center assistantships.

Charlie and Annaley's vision of keeping their family together through the annual foundation meeting has come to fruition. As the children have grown, they've developed their own perspectives on life, religion, and politics. Some are conservative, some are liberal, and others are moderate. Like any family, tension and disagreements sometimes arise when discussing which proposals to fund, where to eat, and life in general. Yet when the dust settles, Kathy, Hardy, Robert, Paul, Maraley, Beverly, Regina, and Becky recognize that their family relationships remain paramount.

Redd Children

Katheryn "Kathy" Anne was born on May 11, 1934, in La Sal, Utah. She attended the local elementary school and Wasatch Academy in Mount Pleasant. After the family moved to Provo, she graduated from BY High in 1952. After enrolling at BYU for three years, she transferred to the University of Minnesota, where she received a degree in American Studies. Upon graduation, she moved to San Francisco for work. She married Gary Mullins, whom she met at Wasatch Academy. The couple has three daughters. The Mullinses lived in Washington and Florida before settling in Sovang, California, where they operated a bookstore and created the Hans Christian Anderson Museum, becoming the first non-Danish individuals to open a business in town. Gary died in 1996, but Kathy continued to operate the bookstore and museum. She was the grand marshal of the 2005 Danish day parade, and the city honored her for her numerous community efforts in 2012.

Charles Hardison "Hardy" was born on June 19, 1936, in Provo, Utah. After attending the La Sal school, he transferred to Wasatch Academy after turning twelve. A year later, the Redd family moved to Provo, and Hardy attended BY High. After he graduated, he attended BYU and then served a mission to Uruguay. When he returned, he attended and graduated from Utah State University. There he met Sonya N. "Sunny" Seely, who taught at North Cache High School. The couple returned to La Sal where Hardy worked for his father. They had ten children. Following in his father's footsteps, he served on the Utah State Legislature from 1979–1985. He was named Forest Landowner of the Year in 2000 by the Utah Forest Stewardship Committee. When the family divided their property holdings, Hardy received the La Sal operation.

Robert Byron was born February 4, 1939, in Moab, Utah. He at-

Left: Kathy Redd Mullins; Right: Hardy and Sunny Redd

tended the local schools until the family moved to Provo when he was in the fifth grade. He graduated from BY High and attended BYU before serving a mission to Finland. His first wife, Heidi Hanson, was a friend of his sister Maraley. Robert and Heidi had two children. Despite Charlie's misgivings, the family voted to allow Robert and Heidi to acquire the Dugout Ranch on Indian Creek where they ran cattle. When Robert and Heidi divorced, they sold the ranch to the Nature Conservancy to preserve the land as open space. Robert lived in Virginia for a time and married Mary Allen. They moved to Provo, where Robert finished a bachelor's degree from BYU in 1992.

Paul David was born on April 29, 1941, in the backside of a mired car near La Sal. He graduated from BY High. He was attending BYU when he joined the army reserve and served a six-month assignment. About that time, his parents met Australian stock raisers in Switzerland, and they invited the Redds to send a son to their country to learn about the sheep industry. Charlie asked twenty-year-old Paul to go. After a year, Paul went to Russia to study livestock husbandry. Paul then served a Latter-day Saint mission to Scotland. When Paul returned, he worked for Charlie, and his responsibilities gradually increased.

Left: Paul and Diane Redd; Right: Robert Redd

Paul married Diane Bowden and they have seven children. When Hardy and Paul split their joint operation, Paul selected the purebred operation and moved to Paradox, Colorado. Paul and Diane continue to raise cattle and host an annual Redd Ranches Bull Sale.

Maraley was born March 2, 1943, in Moab, Utah. She was six years old when the family moved to Provo. She remembers traveling to the Salt Lake Temple at age seven or eight when the Redds received their family sealing or-

Maraley Redd Rasmussen

dinances. She attended BY High and later graduated from Utah State University. Over the years, she worked as Charlie's bookkeeper. Maraley met her husband, Richard Rasmussen, after she graduated from college. Early in their marriage, she taught middle school. The couple has five children. The family traveled with Richard's air force assignments. Wherever they lived, Maraley liked to immerse herself in the culture. For example, she lived in a thatched roof home in England. Eventually the family settled in the Chicago area, where Maraley and Richard have lived for forty years. Maraley has participated in community projects to assist inner-city children and the blind.

Beverly was born May 12, 1945, in Moab, Utah. She was four when the Redds moved to Provo. Beverly attended BY High and then went to BYU for two years. She then moved to California, where she worked for a year. She moved back to La Sal and worked at the store, where she became reacquainted with Lloyd Woods, who had just returned from military service and was living with his parents. They dated and then married. They adopted three children and now live in Mapleton. Following her father's example, Beverly worked as a mail carrier. She has taught piano and played in church meetings. Despite some tragic experiences, she is very positive and kind. She is a loving and caring daughter, wife, and mother who is always willing to help others. Beverly plays a prominent role for the Charles Redd Foundation by working with the applicants and disbursing the annual grants.

Regina was born September 21, 1946. She married James "Jim" Mitchell, Paul's friend from BY High who worked at the ranch one summer. They had five children. After Jim served in the army, they returned to Utah. He found a job with the telephone company and worked for the industry as it changed over his career. They raised their family primarily in Holliday, Utah, but lived in Missouri during the Vietnam War when their first child was born. Regina enjoys diversity of people and culture. She served as a Young Women's president in the Church at a young age and has had served in Church positions throughout her life. She was able to stay home and care for her children and husband. More recently, Regina and James have lived in North Salt Lake and the St. George area.

Rebecca "Becky" Sue was born September 15, 1950, in Monticello, Utah. Although the family had moved to Provo, Annaley stayed

Redd sisters Becky, Gina, and Bev at the 2019 Redd Bull Sale

behind until Becky was born. Becky attended BY High and BYU. She married one of her classmates, Brian Lambert, and they have five children. While Brian attended physical therapy school, the Lamberts lived in Philadelphia. Becky shares her mother's talent for meticulous homemaking and makes delicious bread and meals, which she often shares with others. Becky is also a prize-winning quilter and judge. A prize-winning quilt inspired by Annaley was displayed at the Springville Art Museum, where Becky also gave a quilt trunk talk. She has belonged to quilt guilds and travels to quilt shows. Becky and her family lived in Mapleton on five acres she enjoyed sharing with her grandchildren, but the Lamberts moved to a new home in Springville after Brian retired. They hope to build a yurt on their summer range property in Colorado. Becky enjoys sharing her many talents with her community and church.

LEMUEL HARDISON REDD JR., ELIZA WESTOVER, AND LUCY ZINA LYMAN

Lemuel "Lem" Hardison Redd Jr. was born in Spanish Fork, Utah, on October 25, 1856, to Lemuel Hardison Redd Sr. and Keziah Jane Butler. His parents helped settle southern Utah and moved to New Harmony when Lem was six. He spent his childhood at John D. Lee's small farm with his nine brothers and sisters. From a young age, he worked side by side with his brothers and sisters to build their home. One job involved carrying mud to fill in the chinking and holes in the log cabin. As a family, they raised or grew everything they ate and traded what they made. Lem harvested crops and tended to the animals, especially the cows. His responsibilities included milking, making cheese, and churning butter. Lem was a quiet, sober boy who took life seriously. Sorely needed on the farm, he only attended one winter quarter of formal schooling, walking a mile and a half each way. Reading came naturally to him, and although he was not formally educated, he read everything he could get his hands on.[1]

Around age twenty, Lem attended the University of Deseret (present-day University of Utah) to become a teacher. While there he met his sweetheart, Eliza Ann "Lizzie" Westover, and they dated and became close friends. Lizzie excelled in her studies and was bright and talented. Lem, too, raced through his classes and finished his training in one year. Upon completion, Lem accepted a job as teacher at the New Harmony school. His older sister Jane was one of his students. She recalled: "Well do I remember when a group of [town rowdies] ganged up on him and defied his authority. They were going to run the teacher out, so they said. How surprised and relieved I was, and how frightened too, to see him pitch the ringleader out of the door, down the steps and on his head into the snow! There was no further trouble from [that] source."[2]

Lem's sweetheart Lizzie graduated from the University of Deseret and received employment as a teacher in Pinto, Utah. He visited

Lemuel Hardison Redd Jr.

135

her as often as possible and usually brought his sister Jane along. Lem and Lizzie married in the St. George Temple on April 11, 1878, and had eight children: Lulu, Hattie, Lemuel H., Herbert, Edith, Charles "Charlie," Marion, and Amy. Shortly thereafter, Lem gave up teaching and became a butcher. He and his friend Charley Westover started a butcher shop and sold their slaughtered hogs at the Silver Reef Mining Camp in Nevada.

Eliza Ann Westover Redd

In 1879, Redd and his family were called to the San Juan Mission. They willingly left their home and prosperous butcher shop behind to answer the call to blaze a wagon route to the San Juan River and settle the area. Lem, Eliza, little Lulu, Lem's brother Monroe, and Lemuel Hardison Redd Sr. began their journey, carving a route from Escante to the Colorado River gorge, crossing hundreds of miles of arduous terrain with the additional challenge of winter snowfall and freezing temperatures. Moreover, the journey took three times longer than anticipated and their meager supplies quickly disappeared. Even more challenging was the descent through Hole-in-the-Rock to descend down to the Colorado River gorge. As difficult as that descent was, the pioneers still had two-thirds of the route to go. Before arriving at their destination, another formidable obstacle loomed—ascending San Juan Hill and Comb Ridge. They finally descended the steep grade to the San Juan River Valley, where they erected Bluff Fort and Montezuma Fort eighteen miles upstream. The pioneers dug irrigation systems and eventually founded towns, including Bluff, Blanding, and Monticello. The trek produced a bond among those who had sacrificed so much in the exodus.[3]

Lem Redd's family began a new life for themselves. They built a home and became prominent members of the local civic and church communities. Redd was called as a counselor to Bishop Jens Nielsen and held that position until Redd was called as bishop of the Bluff con-

Lemuel H. Redd Jr. and Eliza Anne Westover Redd home in Bluff City, Utah, ca. 1881

gregation when Nielsen died twenty years later. Lizzie served in the primary and as stake Relief Society president. Lem served as superintendent of the Sunday School, secretary of the Young Men's Mutual Improvement Association, and ward clerk. He later served faithfully as San Juan Stake President from 1910 until his death in 1923. He also found time to hold prominent positions in the community. He was the first assessor and collector for the city of Bluff and was elected to represent his district in the Utah State Legislature.

Lem, also known as L.H. Redd, had an eye for business and was thoroughly invested in seeing San Juan County grow and prosper. His many business ventures included raising sheep and cattle. He borrowed a great deal of money to finance his endeavors. The secured loans that exist today were not part of business arrangements in the 1890s; he simply assured his lenders he would pay back every penny. They trusted him, and he never betrayed that trust. Because of his honesty and integrity, he received their respect and their patronage. Throughout his career, he played a role in the cooperative stores in Bluff, Monticello, and Grayson, as well as in the San Juan-Dolores telephone system, the State Bank of San Juan, the Blanding Irrigation Company, and the La Sal Livestock Company. Lem acted as the financial backbone and one of the most prominent founders of San Juan County.

On October 31, 1883, Lem was sealed in the St. George Temple to his second wife, Lucy Zina Lyman. They had four children together: Carlie, L. Frank, Amasa Jay, and Annie. Lucy sometimes called "Aunt Lucy" was a strong and capable woman and occupied a room in the house Lem, Lizzie, and their children lived in. After Lem and Lucy had their first child, Lucy fled to Mancos, Colorado, to hide from federal marshals. After her second child, L. Frank, was born, Lucy moved back to Bluff and into her own one-room house.

Because of Lem's many vocational, ecclesiastical, and civic responsibilities, his wives made sure things ran smoothly in their homes. Lizzie was an excellent housekeeper and cook, and Lucy was resourceful and efficient. She spun the wool from their sheep to make yarn, which she transformed into beautiful quilts and mattresses. She was a good cook, especially known for her homemade candy and honey cake. She kept bees and extracted the honey. She planted an orchard and a large garden. She canned and preserved her fruits and vegetables and made laundry soap from grease and tallow. Lucy moved to Grayson (Blanding) in 1907 and was active in the Relief Society.

Lemuel Hardison Redd Jr. lived an honorable life. Those who knew him remember his as a man of character and integrity. A deeply spiritual man, his friends and family recall his reverence, humility, and powerful prayers. Presidents Heber J. Grant and George Albert Smith

Lucy Zina Lyman Redd

both spoke of their high regard for him and his "unquestioning faith in the Gospel."[4] Lem passed away on June 1, 1923, in San Juan County, Utah, after contracting influenza. Lucy passed away in Blanding on January 4, 1930. Lizzie lived fifteen years after her husband's death before passing away peacefully in Salt Lake City on March 17, 1938.

1   For biographical material, see Hole-in-the-Rock Foundation, "Lemuel Hardison Redd Jr.," "Eliza Ann Westover Redd," and "Lucy Zina Lyman Redd," accessed 6 February 2021, http://www.hirf.org/; Jesse L. Embry, *La Sal Reflections: A Redd Family Journal* (Provo, UT: Charles Redd Foundation, 1984); Andrew Jenson, ed., *Latter-day Saint Biographical Encyclopedia: A Compilations of Biographical Sketches of Prominent Men and Women in the Church of Jesus Christ of Latter-Day Saints* (Salt Lake City: D.U.P. Memorial Foundation Publishers, 1901); Cornelia Adams Perkins, Marian Gardner Nielson, and Lenora Butt Jones, *Saga of San Juan* (Monticello, Utah: San Juan County Daughters of Pioneers, 1957); Amasa Jay Redd, ed., and Albert R. Lyman, *Lemuel Hardison Redd, Jr. (1856–1923): Pioneer, Leader, Builder* (Salt Lake City: privately published, 1967); Lura Redd, *The Utah Redds and Their Progenitors* (Salt Lake City: Amasa Jay Redd, 1973); Faun McConkie Tanner, *The Far Country: A Regional History of Moab and La Sal, Utah* (Salt Lake City: Olympus Publishing Company, 1976).

2   Redd and Lyman, *Lemuel Hardison Redd, Jr. (1856–1923): Pioneer, Leader, Builder*, 150.

3   Leonard J. Arrington and Davis Bitton, "Lemuel H. Redd: Down the Chute to San Juan," *Saints Without Halos: The Human Side of Mormon History* (Salt Lake City: Signature Books, 1981); Hole-in-the-Rock Foundation, "Lemuel Hardison Redd Sr. Biography," accessed 6 February 2021, http://www.hirf.org/history-bio-Redd-Lemuel-H-Sr.asp.; David E. Miller, *Hole-in-the-Rock: An Epic in the Colonization of the Great American West* (Salt Lake City: University of Utah Press, 1966); Redd and Lyman, *Lemuel Hardison Redd, Jr. (1856–1923)*.

4   Embry, *La Sal Reflections: A Redd Family Journal*, 109.

LEMUEL HARDISON REDD SR., KEZIAH JANE BUTLER, AND SARAH LOUISA CHAMBERLAIN

Lemuel Hardison Redd Sr. was born on July 31, 1836, in Snead's Ferry, Onslow County, North Carolina, to John Hardison Sr. and Elizabeth Hancock Redd.[1] Lemuel was the sixth of eight children: Edward, Harriet (died in infancy), Ann Moriah, Elizabeth Anne, Mary Catherine, John Holt, and Benjamin Jones. At an early age Lemuel was given a body servant named Luke, the son of Elizabeth Hancock's maid Venus.[2]

When Lemuel was two years old in 1838, his family moved to Murfreesboro, Tennessee, and purchased a large plantation and a few African American slaves. Four years later, his family joined The Church of Jesus Christ of Latter-day Saints and his father was baptized by John D. Lee. After deciding to immigrate to the Great Basin to join the body of the Saints, his father legally freed their enslaved persons through an act of the court. Several women and children of Elizabeth's, including Venus and Luke, chose to remain with the family after gaining their freedom.[3]

Redd and his family made the arduous journey to the Salt Lake Valley in 1850 with the James Pace Company. The Redds had been neighbors with the Paces in Murfreesboro. During the 1850 trek, a cholera outbreak claimed the lives of many members in the James Pace Company. Fifty-year-old John and his fourteen-year-old son Lemuel both contracted the disease but fortunately recovered. Lemuel did a man's work on the trek and helped drive the ox team. Upon their arrive in the Salt Lake Valley, the Redds ventured south and established a home and constructed a sawmill in Spanish Fork, Utah.

Lemuel was baptized a member of The Church of Jesus Christ of Latter-day Saints on June 2, 1852, by W. W. Wellis and ordained to the office of priest on the same day. He remained faithful to his duties as a priesthood holder throughout his life. He was part of a militia of several thousand soldiers organized by President Brigham Young to prepare for conflict if

Lemuel Haridson Redd Sr.

the US army attacked the Saints during the Utah War. He was called upon to defend frontier settlements during the Walker War and the Black Hawk War. Unfortunately, the Redds' sawmill was destroyed during the Walker War and they eventually moved to Palmyra to start again.[4]

Bishop William Pace performed the marriage of Lemuel Redd Sr.

Keziah Jane Butler Redd

and Keziah Jane Butler on January 2, 1856. They received their endowments and sealing ordinances at the hand of Daniel H. Wells, counselor to Brigham Young, the following year. Lemuel "Pap" and Keziah had thirteen children together, ten of whom lived to adulthood—Lemuel Hardison Jr., Mary Jane, John Wilson, William Alexander, James Monroe, Caroline Elizabeth, Amos Thorton (died in infancy), Moriah Luella, Charity Alvira, and Alice. Shortly after their marriage, church leaders called Lemuel and Keziah to the Las Vegas Mission to help settle Las Vegas, Nevada, and attempt to mine lead. When the mining proved fruitless and the mission disbanded, they returned for a few years to Spanish Fork, three weeks before the birth of their first son, Lemuel "Lem" or "L.H." Hardison Jr. In 1862, President Brigham Young asked Lemuel and Keziah to settle New Harmony, Utah, south of Cedar City. They took their young family with four small children and built a new life. Redd quickly emerged as a town leader, serving in the civil government and as a member of the county court.

Sarah Louisa Chamberlain worked as a mother's helper to Keziah. When the time came for Lemuel to marry a second wife, Keziah chose Sarah Louisa because she liked her and knew they could get along. After Lemuel's marriage to Sarah Louisa in October 1866, Keziah and Sarah Louisa shared not only a husband but also a house for the next four years. Lemuel and Sarah Louisa had fourteen children, although two died in infancy. Their children included Moriah Vilate (died in infancy), Solomon (died in infancy), Wayne Hardison, Benjamin Franklin, Terresa Artemisia, Lemuel Burton, George Edwin, Susan Elizabeth, Parley, John Wiley, Jenny May, Effie, Ancil Ray, and Hazel Lurena. Each of Lemuel's children recalled days spent in the canyons, gathering and roasting pine nuts, horseback riding, camping trips, and other things that please children. Lemuel enjoyed seeing his children happy.

In the fall of 1879, Lemuel, James Monroe, Lem, and Lem's wife and daughter joined a group of 250 pioneers called by church leaders to colonize the San Juan River Valley in southeastern Utah. These pioneer families arrived at the banks of the Colorado River as cold temperatures and snow commenced. Lemuel Sr. and three others scouted the road ahead. Unfortunately, there was no road, and the rough terrain made wagon

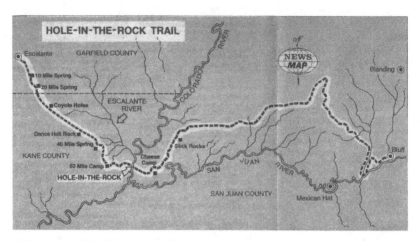

Hole-in-the Rock-Trail, Courtesy Dick Carter, Deseret News

travel difficult, if not impossible. On Christmas night, frozen and hungry, Lemuel had a dream that showed them the way to travel to the San Juan River. After watching three desert bighorn leap down a steep ledge, the men envisioned they could get the families down safely through Hole-in-the-Rock. Through divine intervention, the Hole-in-the-Rock pioneers made it safely to San Juan. [5] Shortly thereafter, Lemuel received letters from his family stating they were sick and in distress, so he returned home to care for his wives and children. Upon arriving home, he found seven of his children suffering from diphtheria.

The 1882 Edmunds Bill banned the practice of plural marriage. The bill also meant anyone caught practicing polygamy would be arrested. Lemuel had been sealed for time and all eternity to Keziah and Sarah Louisa, and he did not intend to desert either of them due to the new congressional law. For months at a time, Lemuel lived in hiding to evade federal marshals. During the summer of 1887, two marshals invaded his New Harmony home. Hoping to find Lemuel and Sarah Louisa cohabiting so they could arrest him, the marshals made a surprise visit. Sarah Louisa had been warned they were coming and hid in the willows nearby. Feeling they had been outwitted, they could do nothing but subpoena Luella and Wayne, who afterwards appeared in court to testify against their father. They told their story in a straightforward way, but the marshals did not get the satisfaction they wanted. Lemuel was under two indictments and the penalty for each was six months in prison and a $300 fine. Lemuel moved Sarah Louisa and the family to Bluff to escape scrutiny in New Harmony.

After a few more years of evading surveillance, Lemuel moved Sarah Louisa and the children to Colonia Juarez, Mexico, in 1891. From this time forward, he divided his time between his families in Utah and Mexico. In 1895, Redd was in Mexico when he received word that Keziah was terribly ill, so he rushed to Utah as quickly as possible. After four months

Sarah Louisa Chamberlain Redd

of illness, his beloved Keziah passed away on May 15, 1895. Her children spoke of her as devoted, brave, noble, generous, and saintly. They claimed truthfully that no harsh word ever fell from their mother's lips, as she lived by her motto "Better suffer wrong than do wrong."[6]

Throughout his life, Lemuel held numerous church positions including that of bishopric counselor, and he served as a high priest and a seventy. In 1902, Lemuel attended general conference in Salt Lake City and was ordained a patriarch.

On March 9, 1907, Sarah Louisa passed away. Three months later, in June, Lemuel suffered a serious accident from which he never fully recovered. He lived with his daughter Artemisia following the accident until he was able to return to his home in Mexico. Lemuel Hardison Redd Sr. passed away on June 9, 1910, in Colonia Juarez. At the time of his death, he had twenty living children, 104 grandchildren, and many great-grandchildren.

1 Lura Redd, *The Utah Redds and Their Progenitors* (Salt Lake City: Amasa Jay Redd, 1973), 25.

2 John H. and Elizabeth Redd immigrated to Utah Territory from Tennessee, bringing six freed African Americans formerly belonging to Elizabeth with them. Redd, *The Utah Redds and Their Progenitors*, 25, 197.

3 Tonya Reiter, "Redd Slave Histories: Family, Race, and Sex in Pioneer Utah," *Utah Historical Quarterly* 85 no. 2 (Spring 2017): 109–26.

4 For biographical information about Lemuel Hardison Redd Sr., see: "History of Lemuel Hardison Redd," unpublished history, Daughters of the Utah Pioneers, Salt Lake City, Utah; Kate B. Carter, ed., *Our Pioneer Heritage,* vols. 8 and 18 (Salt Lake City, UT: Daughters of Utah Pioneers, 1958–1977); Carol Ivans Collett, "Lemuel Hardison Redd, Pioneer of 1850," unpublished history, Daughters of the Utah Pioneers, Salt Lake City, Utah; Jesse L. Embry, *La Sal Reflections: A Redd Family Journal* (Provo, UT: Charles Redd Foundation, 1984); Andrew Jenson, ed., *Latter-day Saint Biographical Encyclopedia: A Compilations of Biographical Sketches of Prominent Men and Women in the Church of Jesus Christ of Latter-Day Saints* (Salt Lake City: D.U.P. Memorial Foundation Publishers, 1901), reprint available digitally through Brigham Young University; Regina Redd Mitchell, "Lemuel Hardison Redd," ca. 1986, unpublished history from the files of the Daughters of the Utah Pioneers, Salt Lake City, Utah; Cornelia Adams Perkins, Marian Gardner Nielson, and Lenora Butt Jones, *Saga of San Juan* (Monticello, UT: San Juan County Daughters of Pioneers, 1957).

5 "In all the annals of the West, replete with examples of courage, tenacity and ingenuity, there is no better example of the indomitable pioneer spirit than that of the Hole-In-the-Rock expedition of the San Juan Mission. No pioneer company ever build a wagon road through wilder, rougher, more inhospitable country, still one of the least-known regions of American. None ever demonstrated more courage, faith, and devotion to a cause than this group." David E. Miller, *Hole-in-the-Rock: An Epic in the Colonization of the Great American West* (Salt Lake City: University of Utah Press, 1966), ix. See also, Leonard J. Arrington, and Davis Bitton, "Lemuel H. Redd: Down the Chute to San Juan," *Saints Without Halos: The Human Side of Mormon History* (Salt Lake City: Signature Books, 1981); Hole-in-the-Rock Foundation, "Lemuel Hardison Redd Sr. Biography," accessed 6 February 2021, http://www.hirf.org/history-bio-Redd-Lemuel-H-Sr.asp.; Amasa Jay Redd, ed., and Albert R. Lyman, *Lemuel Hardison Redd, Jr. (1856–1923): Pioneer, Leader, Builder* (Salt Lake City: privately published, 1967); Faun McConkie Tanner, *The Far Country: A Regional History of Moab and La Sal, Utah* (Salt Lake City: Olympus Publishing Company, 1976).

6   Lemuel Hardison Redd, as directed to his daughter, ed. by Jessie L. Embry, "Life Sketch of Lemuel Hardison Redd," *La Sal Reflections* (Provo, UT: Charles Redd Foundation, 1984), 100.

JOHN HARDISON REDD SR. AND ELIZABETH HANCOCK

John Hardison Redd Sr. was born on December 27, 1799, at Stump Sound, Onslow County, North Carolina, to Whittaker Redd and Elizabeth Harrison. His father's first wife, Nancy Cary died, leaving a daughter, Mary, born September 27, 1792. Whitaker married Elizabeth Hardison. Together they had a son, John Hardison Redd Jr. Elizabeth died shortly thereafter and an African American nanny cared for John and Mary. Whitaker remarried a third time when John was about five years old, and a third sibling joined their blended family.[1]

Not much is known of John's childhood, but his professional interests and skills were many and varied. Court minutes and records mention John frequently as a buyer, seller, juror, guardian, etc. He was active in business, community, and judicial affairs. At one point, John was a sea captain and carried a sword and scabbard. He had specialty-colored eyeglasses he wore while at sea that had hinged blue lenses worn either in front of the eye or alongside the temple. There are legends that John traded as far as Barbados in the West Indies.

John left the sea to become a Tennessee planter. He bought, owned, and operated a plantation about fifteen or twenty miles from Murfreesboro. John's relatives operated sawmills and passed along their knowledge to him. He, in turn, conveyed this information about farming and construction to his son Lemuel. John had excellent penmanship, better than most of his contemporaries, although his sister Mary could not even sign her own name. He wrote various literary works, including a ballad about his conversion for his daughter Mary.

John married Elizabeth Hancock on March 2, 1826, in Sneads Ferry, North Carolina, and they had eight children together: Harriet, Edward Ward, Ann Moriah, Ann Elizabeth, Mary Catherine, Lemuel Hardison (Sr.), John Holt, and Benjamin Reed. Elizabeth was born to Zebedee Hancock and Abigail Taylor on January 25, 1798, and was their only living daughter. Elizabeth also had two brothers, William and Anson. Elizabeth's family owned enslaved Africans, and her father's will bequeathed her an African American woman named Venus, who lived with Elizabeth for the rest of her life. Elizabeth worked hard in the home and was kept busy laundering bedding and clothing, weaving, sewing, cooking, knitting, etc. Anything the family needed was done by hand in the home.

John and Elizabeth joined The Church of Jesus Christ of Latter-day Saints on June 17, 1843, baptized by John D. Lee. John Hardison Redd was a heavy user of tobacco, but he gave up the habit after his conversion.[2] John received a patriarchal blessing from Church Patriarch Hyrum Smith on April 3, 1844. A few years after the Prophet Joseph Smith's martyrdom in June 1844, John sold his land and freed his slaves by action of the court in preparation to immigrate to the Great Basin. Elizabeth also freed her slaves. Two African American women, Venus and Chaney, and their four children chose to stay with the Redds, joining the hegira of Saints migrating west.[3] John's Tennessee neighbor, James Pace, was captain over the fourth company to cross the plains in 1850. During the 1850 trek, a cholera outbreak claimed the lives of many members in the James Pace Company. Fifty-year-old John and his son Lemuel both contracted the disease but fortunately recovered. John kept a daily journal of their travels in a little notebook he made out of long sheets of paper folded and sewn together with twine.[4]

They arrived in Utah Territory and moved to the Spanish Fork area. As in North Carolina and Tennessee, John was very active in civic and church affairs; once settled in Spanish Fork, John became justice of the peace on November 24, 1854. John and Elizabeth suffered a series of tragedies when two of their children died within two years of each other. First, Mary Catherine passed away on May 5, 1851, at the age of 17, and then John Holt was thrown from a horse and died on November 25, 1853, at the age of 15. As a mother, Elizabeth was heartbroken to have lost two children in so short a time. She died just three days after John Holt's accident on November 28, 1853, reputably of a broken heart.

Three years later, on May 2, 1856, John Hardison, fifty-seven, married Mary Lewis, who was just seventeen. She was born November 22, 1839, in Alsmorgan, Wales, and was the daughter of John A. Lewis and Ann John. John and Mary had one child together, Mary Ann, who was born August 28, 1857. In 1858, John was kicked by a horse. They sent to Salt Lake City for a doctor, but John died before the doctor could arrive. John Hardison Redd died June 15, 1858, in Spanish Fork, Utah. He was buried in the Redd graveyard (now known as the Pioneer Cemetery) with other members of his family.[5]

1 Another account places his birth at Sneads Ferry, Onslow County, North Carolina. Lura Redd, *The Utah Redds and Their Progenitors* (Salt Lake City: Amasa Jay Redd, 1973), 175–275.

2 Redd, *The Utah Redds and Their Progenitors*, 187.

3 Redd, *The Utah Redds and Their Progenitors*, 197. Tonya Reiter, "Redd Slave Histories: Family, Race, and Sex in Pioneer Utah," *Utah Historical Quarterly* 85 no. 2 (Spring 2017): 109–26.

4 Transcript for John H. Redd Diary, June–August 1850.

5 Redd, *The Utah Redds and Their Progenitors*, 228.

JOHN TOPHAM AND SUSAN REDD BUTLER ENDOWMENT

Descendants of the Redd family have continued to generously support the Redd Center through the creation of the John Topham and Susan Redd Butler Endowment:

John Lowe Butler I and Caroline Skeen
John Lowe Butler II and Nancy Smith
John Topham Butler and Susan Redd
Karl Butler and Mollie Parker
William Howard Peters and Hazel Butler

John Lowe Butler I and Caroline Skeen

John Lowe Butler I was born April 8, 1808, to James Butler and Charity Lowe in Warren County, Kentucky, and spent his childhood on the family farm in rural Kentucky. Severe illness followed by continued poor health and several accidents hampered his growing years, and John was lucky to reach adulthood.[1] John married Caroline Farozine Skeen, the daughter of middle-class, slave-owning farmers, on February 3, 1831, and they became the parents of twelve children.[2] The Butlers were introduced to The Church of Jesus Christ of Latter-day Saints by missionaries in 1835, and their subsequent conversion caused irreparable rifts with Caroline's family. [3] After joining the church, John practiced polygamy and married seven additional wives. The family followed the saints to Missouri and then Illinois, where John was one of twelve men from the Nauvoo Legion designated as Joseph Smith's bodyguards.[4] From there, the Butlers continued west with the Saints and arrived in the Salt Lake Valley in the fall of 1852. Eventually, John and his large family settled in Spanish Fork where he served as a bish-op and active member of the community.[5] Due to cardiovascular dam-age caused by severe illness during his childhood, John died relatively young at age fifty-two.[6]

John Lowe Butler II and Nancy Smith

John Lowe Butler II was born February 28, 1844, to John Lowe But-ler I and Caroline Farozine Skeen in Nauvoo, Illinois. The joy of his birth was overshadowed by the pain resulting from the martyrdom of the Prophet Joseph Smith and the hardships that followed. The But-lers were driven from their Nauvoo homes by mobs. They joined the wagon companies of other Latter-day Saint refugees headed into the frontier of Iowa and Nebraska. The family arrived in Salt Lake on Oc-tober 16, 1852, and eventually settled in Spanish Fork, where John II was baptized. He married Nancy Franzetta Smith on June 23, 1873. She was sickly as a child and struggled with poor health. When they became engaged, it was thought she might not live very long, but he told her that he was willing to take her as his bride even if they could only have a year of life together. They became the parents of ten chil-dren. John II married a second wife, Sarah Johnson, on April 10, 1882, and they had six children together. On December 30, 1898, John Lowe Butler II died at Richfield of Bright's disease at age fifty-four.[7]

John Topham Butler and Susan Redd

John Topham Butler was born in 1879 in Parowan, Utah, the third child of James Butler and Charlotte Topham. The family lived on a small farm and John T. spent most of his youth riding his pony in and around Richfield, Utah. He moved to the Latter-day Saint colonies in Mexico in 1900 and met his future wife, Susan Elizabeth Redd, in Colonia Juarez. They were married in 1902 and had seven children. John T. freighted goods, labored in the mines, and helped construct a railroad. The family moved to Douglas, Arizona, in 1906, where he helped build the town's first chapel. John T. also volunteered with the local fire department and was a boilermaker at the new Douglas Phelps-Dodge Smelter. Later, the Butlers moved to Lehi, Arizona, where John T. owned a country store, farmed in the area, and continued his church service. He died in Mesa,

Arizona, in 1940 while working in his orchard.[8]

Susan Elizabeth Redd was born on December 14, 1880, in Harmony, Utah, to Lemuel Hardison Redd Sr. and his second wife, Sariah Louisa Chamberlain Redd. Her childhood was spent working with and learning from her mother—doing household chores, baking bread and pies, and making the family's clothing.

Lemuel decided to move with his second wife to the Mormon colonies in Mexico to escape the US Marshals. Susan helped her mother with new babies and attended school in Colonia Juarez. She met John T. at a dance in 1899, and they courted through correspondence until they married in 1902.[9] After they were married, the couple traded milk to a neighbor in exchange for piano lessons for Susan. She would go on to play the organ and the piano at the Temple Information Center well into her eighties.[10] When her husband passed away, she took in boarders to support her five unmarried children. She died in Mesa, Arizona, in 1977.[11]

John Topham Butler and Susan Elizabeth Redd

Karl Butler and Mollie Parker

Karl Douglas Butler was born in 1910, in Douglas, Arizona, and was the fourth child of John Topham and Susan Elizabeth Redd Butler. Even as a child, Karl showed an interest in plants and how they functioned.[12] He graduated from the University of Arizona in 1932 and completed a master's degree in plant pathology in 1933. He pursued additional graduate studies at Iowa State College and Cornell University. In 1938, he met Mollie Emerson Parker of Reading, Massachusetts, at a Gamma Alpha dance. Mollie had just graduated from Simmons College with a degree in general science and was employed at Cornell as an assistant professor for the foods and nutrition courses. Mollie was a strong supporter and collaborator of the College of Veterinary Medicine at Cornell University. She was particularly interested in research on herd socialization, parasite management, and reproductive studies.[13]

Karl and Mollie were married on September 9, 1939, in the Church of the Shepherd and then later sealed in the Mesa Arizona Temple. They were the devoted parents of five children.[14] In 1940, Karl completed a PhD in plant pathology and Mollie completed a master's in nutrition, both from Cornell. Karl's first post-graduate assignment was in Costa Rica and the Amazon, where he worked on developing a new rubber source.[15] Based on his work and research, he was appointed by President Dwight E. Eisenhower as an Assistant to the US Secretary of Agriculture, Ezra Taft Benson.[16] As a researcher and farming consultant, Karl Butler traveled

Karl Butler ca. 1948

throughout the world with his wife, improving agricultural practices.

Karl was also very interested in history. He oversaw the Peter Whitmer farm, wrote a book with Richard E. Palmer on Brigham Young's experiences in New York, and was very supportive of the Redd Center. In 1985, he provided funding for an endowment that he requested be named after his parents. Mollie passed away in 1992 and Karl died in Ithaca, New York, in 2002.[17]

The Karl and Mollie Butler family ca. 1978. Left to right: Linda, Doug, Karl, Mollie, John, Don, and Bob

William Howard Peters and Hazel Butler

Hazel Butler was born in 1912, in Douglas, Arizona, and was the fifth child of John Topham and Susan Elizabeth Redd Butler. As a young child, her health was poor, but she did well in school despite this. She graduated from the Arizona State Teachers College (now Arizona State University) in 1934 and taught school in Mesa, Arizona, for eleven years. Hazel met William Howard Peters in 1941 in Phoenix, Arizona. Howard had recently graduated in Business Administration from Stanford University, but after the attack on Pearl Harbor, he felt it was his duty to volunteer for military service. He was accepted into officer's training school and served in the air force on the Pacific Front from

1942–1945. When he returned, he and Hazel were married in Pasadena, California, and had two children together. Hazel was active in the community and served on the PTA for sixteen years. She was also the first den mother for the Latter-day Saint Cub Scouts of Glendale, California. Howard served as a city council member and mayor of Glendale in the 1960s.[18] Howard and Hazel made a substantial gift of property to the Charles Redd Center for Western Studies. This and other financial contributions helped fund the research endowments. Howard passed away in 1981, and Hazel in 1995.[19]

Above: Hazel and William Howard Peters on their wedding day, 1945

Hazel and William Howard Peters and their children, Susan June and Dennis Edwin, 1961

1   William Hartley, *My Best for the Kingdom: History and Autobiography of John Lowe Butler, a Mormon Frontiersman* (Salt Lake City, UT: Aspen Books, 1993), 2–3. John Lowe Butler's daughter Keziah Butler married Lemuel Hardison Redd, Sr. See, "Autobiography of John Lowe Butler, 1808–1861," unpublished manuscript copy in Charles Redd Center for Western Studies, Brigham Young University, Provo, Utah.

2   Hartley, *My Best for the Kingdom*, 22.

3   Hartley, *My Best for the Kingdom*, 24, 30.

4   Hartley, *My Best for the Kingdom*, 31–33, 87, 119.

5   Hartley, *My Best for the Kingdom*, 269–70.

6   Hartley, *My Best for the Kingdom*, 347.

7   C.S.M. Jones LLC, Family Heritage Consulting, "John Butler." Hole-in-the-Rock Foundation, Bluff Fort Visitor Center. Accessed February 13, 2021, http://www.hirf.org/ButlerJohn.html.

8   Karl Butler, *The Family of John Topham and Susan Elizabeth Redd Butler* (Provo, UT: John Lowe Butler Family Society, 1990), 3–5; Emma Baker Sorensen, comp., *Simon Baker and His Descendants*, Frederick Chester, ed. (Sorensen, UT: Utah Printing Company, 1964).

9   Butler, *The Family of John Topham*, 25–27.

10 Butler, *The Family of John Topham*, 37, 66–67.

11 Butler, *The Family of John Topham*, 57–59, 67.

12 Butler, *The Family of John Topham*, 131.

13 Butler, *The Family of John Topham*, 139–41.

14 Butler, *The Family of John Topham*, 144.

15 Butler, *The Family of John Topham*, 141–43.

16 Butler, *The Family of John Topham*, 148.

17 "Karl and Mollie Butler," BYU Charles Redd Center for Western Studies, accessed February 20, 2021. https://reddcenter.byu.edu/Pages/karl-and-mollie-butler.

18 Butler, *The Family of John Topham*, 159–63.

19 Butler, *The Family of John Topham*, 166–67; Sorensen and Sorensen, eds., *Simon Baker and His Descendants*.

BERTIS L. AND ANNA E. C. EMBRY FAMILY ENDOWMENT

Jessie L. Embry and her parents, Bertis L. and Anna Elizabeth Coulson Embry, funded this endowment. Bertis L. Embry was born on November 23, 1914, in Tipton County, Tennessee. He moved with his parents to Texas, Arkansas, and Arizona before the family settled in North Ogden, Utah. After attending Weber State College, he served a Latter-day Saint mission in Germany in the 1930s, just as Adolph Hitler took power. He returned and completed a bachelor's degree in agricultural engineering from Utah State University.

Bertis married Anna Elizabeth Coulson on June 6, 1941. After their marriage, they traveled with a Rural Electric Administration tent show teaching farmers how to use electric equipment. When World War II started, Bertis worked briefly for the Manhattan Project before joining the navy. He returned to Cache Valley, where he taught drafting and engineering classes to returning war veterans at Utah State University. He received an engineering degree from Stanford University and a PhD from

Bertis and Anna Embry

the University of Missouri. Bertis was an electrical engineering professor at Utah State and specialized in irrigation, agricultural, and electronic engineering. He worked for the United States Agency for International Development (USAID) in Iran and Guatemala.

Anna was born May 16, 1915, in Nephi, Utah. She trained as a nurse at the Holy Cross Hospital in Salt Lake City, Utah. She was working as a nurse at the Logan Hospital when she met Bertis on a blind date. She was a homemaker during most of her married life. She returned to work as a nurse while Bertis completed his PhD. Afterwards, she continued to work at a nursing home and as a public health nurse in Cache County. She traveled with her husband and their five children for his work assignments. Bertis and Anna served a Latter-day Saint mission in Barcelona, Spain.

As her parents aged, Jessie helped care for them. After Bertis died in 1999, Anna lived with Jessie until her death in 2003. As supportive parents, the Embrys gave money to the Redd Center to assist their daughter's projects. Initially, the Embry endowment provided funding for oral history projects. Later, that was expanded to include topics of interest to the Embry family, including Latter-day Saint and Utah connections with the Middle East and Latin America, Utah nursing programs, Latter-day Saint ethnic studies, and the Mormon History Association.

CLARENCE DIXON TAYLOR FAMILY ENDOWMENT

Clarence Dixon Taylor—nicknamed "Bud" to his mother's chagrin—was born on May 11, 1909, to Arthur Nicholls and Maria Louise Dixon Taylor, the sixth of eight children.[1] As a young boy, Taylor's parents taught him the value of hard work, and he helped with the planting and cared for the animals. He and his family enjoyed taking advantage of cooler canyon temperatures and spent summers at the Wildwood cabin. Their favorite cabin activities included sliding down the old "devil's slide," swimming, and playing softball and croquet.[2] After graduating from high school, Taylor attended BYU, where he was elected student body vice-president.[3] When his call to the California Mission arrived in 1930, his mother paid a visit to President Heber J. Grant to explain that there must have been a mistake because he should be going to South Africa. Taylor's call was changed to the South African Mission, and for the rest of his life he carried on his mother's devotion to their South African roots, where her father had joined The Church of Jesus Christ of Latter-day Saints in 1856.[4]

Clarence Dixon Taylor, ca. 1927

Upon completing his missionary service, Taylor returned home and re-enrolled in courses at BYU. In 1936, he graduated with a degree in business management and a minor in economics.[5] Afterwards, he worked with his father and brothers in their furniture business, Dixon-Taylor-Russell Company, until it closed in 1964. He then took care of accounts payable for the BYU Bookstore until he retired in 1974.[6]

World War II interrupted his life, sending him to notable battles of the European theater. As a cannoneer in the 109th Regiment of the 28th Division, Taylor landed on Utah Beach during the invasion of Normandy, fought at the thinnest line of defense and barely escaped capture during the Battle of the Bulge, and fought on into Germany. He would never talk about the war, much to the disappointment of his nephews, but they enjoyed the consolation prize of being gifted his military dress hats.[7] Taylor later wrote, "There is no good that comes from war, other than retaining one's liberty. War only results in destruction, heartache, and sorrow—a period of waste, loss of life, pain, and suffering. To me, a period of time to be forgotten."[8]

Although Taylor never married, his life was devoted to his family in a way that set a standard for all who knew him. He recognized early the value of computers for genealogical work and entered all his family records on an Apple IIe. Before that, he lined his basement with thir-

ty-two lineal feet of 4' x 8' plywood panels with hundreds of relatives' names on small strips of paper. At their weddings, each of his nieces and nephews received a booklet with family group sheets of their ancestors and their own, ready to be continued. His published books include a history of the 1820 settlers of South Africa and two volumes of family records and stories. In 2005, Taylor established a missionary trust fund in memory of his parents. If

Henry Aldous Dixon

a descendant can document their direct relationship to Henry Aldous Dixon, they qualify to receive up to half the cost of their full-time Latter-day Saint mission. Since its inception, more than 250 individuals and couples have received this benefit.[9]

As a veteran, Taylor was eligible to purchase a war surplus jeep in 1945, which he and a cousin, Verl Dixon, picked up at Hill Air Force Base. Uncle Bud's jeep was the envy and pride of the entire extended family and Oak Hills neighborhood. As each niece and nephew got their driver's license, they were allowed to use the jeep for a week. That privilege continued until one of them drove it up the front steps of the high school in Price, Utah. For his ninety-fifth birthday, Taylor's nieces and nephews each wrote a memory of Uncle Bud. Many involved the jeep, and all reflected on his influence for good. Taylor was a quiet, good neighbor and donated his own property for a private neighborhood park in Provo, affectionately known as "Uncle Bud's Park." Clarence Dixon Taylor was a lifelong Provo citizen. He died on May 21, 2005, in the Courtyard at Jamestown Assisted Living Facility in Provo, Utah, just ten days after his 96th birthday. An award at the Charles Redd Center for Western Studies has been named for Clarence Dixon Taylor in recognition of the outstanding contributions the Taylor and Dixon families have made to the economic development of Provo and Central Utah since 1865.[10]

"Uncle Bud's" nephews, left to right: George Taylor, Hank Taylor, John Taylor, and Kenneth Kartchner

1   John Arthur Taylor, Henry Dixon Taylor, Jr., and Kenneth Taylor Kartchner, eds., *Clarence Dixon Taylor: His Life and Work* (Provo, UT: Clarence Dixon Taylor Trust, 2009), ix, 4. See also, Clarence Dixon Taylor, *George Taylor, Sr. (1838–1926) and His Family: Photographer, Merchant, Banker* (Provo, UT: Clarence Dixon Taylor Trust, 1983); Clarence Dixon Taylor, *My Folks, the Dixons* (Provo, UT: Clarence Dixon Taylor Trust, 2 vols. 2nd printing, 1978); John Arthur Taylor, Henry Dixon Taylor, Jr., and Kenneth Taylor Kartchner, eds. *Letters of Maria Dixon Taylor and Clarence Dixon Taylor, 1930–1933, 1943–1945* (Provo: L. Tom Perry Special Collections, Harold B. Lee Library, Brigham Young University, 2011).

2   Taylor, et al., *Clarence Dixon Taylor*, 5–11.

3   Taylor, et al., *Clarence Dixon Taylor*, 17.

4   Taylor, et al., *Clarence Dixon Taylor*, 17. There is a discrepancy between these two sources regarding Clarence's initial mission call. Family Search claims he was called to the England mission before being reassigned to the South African Mission, but *Clarence Dixon Taylor* states he was first called to the California Mission before South Africa.

5   Taylor, et al., *Clarence Dixon Taylor*. 23.

6   "Clarence Dixon Taylor," BYU Charles Redd Center for Western Studies, accessed January 14, 2022. https://reddcenter.byu.edu/Pages/clarence-dixon-taylor.

7   Taylor, et al., *Clarence Dixon Taylor*, 201.

8   "Clarence Dixon Taylor."

9   "Clarence Dixon Taylor."

10 "Clarence Dixon 'Uncle Bud' Taylor," FamilySearch, accessed January 14, 2022. https://www.familysearch.org/tree/person/details/KWC8-BJW.

APPENDIX 1. REDD CENTER PERSONNEL

Directors, Assistant Directors, and Associate Directors

Leonard J. Arrington, Director (1972–1980)

Thomas G. Alexander, Director (1980–1992), Assistant/Associate Director (1972–1980)

Jessie L. Embry, Oral History Program Director (1979–1994), Assistant/Associate Director (1994–2015), Acting Director (June–December 2001, August–December 2002)

William A. Wilson, Director (1992–1996)

Edward A. Geary, Director (1996–2002)

Brian Q. Cannon, Director (2002–2018)

Brenden W. Rensink, Assistant/Associate Director (2015–present)

Jay H. Buckley, Director (2018–present)

Office Staff

Pamela Campbell Su'a	Kris Nelson
Deanne Whitmore	Olga de LaRosa
Barbara Lyman	Kris Nelson
Irene Fuja	Jason E. Thompson
Natalie Ethington	Mary K. Nelson
Jennifer Dean	Amy M. Carlin

Numerous graduate and undergraduate research assistants, interns, oral history interviewers, and transcriptionists have provided valuable assistance in helping the directors with research. Those working in oral history made it possible to create the Redd Center's large set of oral histories.

See Appendix 7: Redd Center Oral History Collection

Top left: Pamela Campbell Su'a; Top right: Kris Nelson; Bottom left: Mary K. Nelson; Bottom right: Amy M. Carlin

APPENDIX 2. REDD CENTER BOARD MEMBERS, 2022

Thomas G. Alexander, Lemuel Hardison Redd Jr. Professor Emeritus of Western American History, Brigham Young University

James B. Allen, Lemuel Hardison Redd Jr. Professor Emeritus of Western American History, Brigham Young University

Val J. Anderson, Department of Plant and Wildlife Sciences, Brigham Young University

Tacey M. Atsitty, Diné, Indigenous Poet

Adam Brown, Department of Political Science, Brigham Young University

Mark Brunson, Department of Environment and Society, Utah State University

John E. Butler, Butler Family Representative

Brian Q. Cannon, Former Redd Center Director and Department of History Chair, Brigham Young University

Dennis Cutchins, Department of English, Brigham Young University

Jessie L. Embry, Redd Center Emeritus, Brigham Young University

Ed Geary, Redd Center and Department of English Emeritus, Brigham Young University

Holly George, *Utah Historical Quarterly*, Utah State Historical Society

Jason B. Jones, Western Museums Association

John M. Murphy, L. Tom Perry Special Collections, Brigham Young

University

Jeff Nichols, Department of History, Westminster College

Samuel Otterstrom, Department of Geography, Brigham Young University

Erik Redd Rasmussen, Redd Family Representative

Carol Ward, Department of Sociology, Brigham Young University

APPENDIX 3. LEMUEL HARDISON REDD JR. PROFESSOR IN WESTERN AMERICAN HISTORY

Endowed Chair

Prominent Utah ranchers and philanthropists Charlie and Annaley Redd established the Lemuel Hardison Redd Jr. Professor in Western American History Endowed Chair in 1972 to promote and honor research, publication, and teaching in western American history. They named the chair in honor of Charlie's father, who settled and developed Latter-day Saint communities in southeastern Utah's red rock desert, forests, and mountains and established a successful livestock empire. Charlie described his father as "a man who lived a big life," a somewhat lonely and enigmatic character with "many admirers who regarded him as a giant."

Endowed Chair Holders

Leonard J. Arrington (1973–1987)

Leonard J. Arrington was born in Twin Falls, Idaho, on July 2, 1917. He grew up in a Latter-day Saint farming household and planned an agricultural career. He attended the University of Idaho, where he studied agricultural science and then later switched to agricultural economics. He completed a PhD in Economics at the University of North Carolina-Chapel Hill in 1952. Trained as an economic historian, Arrington eventually expanded his research into many aspects of history. His revised dissertation, *Great Basin Kingdom: An Economic History of the Latter-day Saints, 1830–1900* was published by Harvard University Press in 1958 and has been a standard for Mormon and western American economic history. Arrington taught at Utah State University until 1973, when he became the first holder of the Lemuel Hardison Redd Jr. Chair of Western History, and the first director of the Charles Redd Center for Western Studies at Brigham Young University. At the same time, he was called as Church Historian for The Church of Jesus Christ of Latter-day Saints. Arrington continued as the Redd Center director until the Church History Division was transferred to BYU. He then became the director of the Joseph Fielding Smith Institute for Church History. He held the Redd Chair until his retirement in 1982. In that capacity, he served as mentor for many practitioners of the new Mormon history.

See chapter 1, especially page 18, for detailed biography.

James B. Allen (1987–1992)

James "Jim" B. Allen was born in Ogden, Utah, on June 14, 1927. His family lived in Coalville and Salt Lake City, Utah, and in Star Valley, Wyoming. When he was eleven, they moved to Logan, Utah. Allen received his bachelor's degree in history from Utah State University in 1954, his master's degree from BYU in 1956, and his PhD in history from the University of Southern California in 1963. He began his professional career in the Church Education System in 1954. He was a seminary teacher, seminary coordinator, institute teacher, and director of the Institutes of Religion in Long Beach and San Bernardino, California. In 1963, he became a member of the church history faculty at Brigham Young University, and the following year he joined the history department. In 1972, he was appointed Assistant Church Historian, working with newly appointed Church Historian Leonard J. Arrington. For the next seven years, Allen spent half his time in that capacity and the other half at BYU. He returned full time to BYU in 1979 and served as chair of the history department from 1981 to 1987, when he was appointed as the Lemuel Hardison Redd Jr. chair. He held this appointment until his retirement in 1992.

Throughout his career, Allen has authored, co-authored, and

co-edited fourteen books and monographs; around ninety articles, mostly related to Latter-day Saint church history; and numerous book reviews in professional journals. He has received several prizes and awards for his work, including the David Woolley Evans and Beatrice Cannon Evans Biography Award in 1986 for *Trials of Discipleship: The Story of William Clayton, a Mormon* (re-published in 2002 as *No Toil nor Labor Fear: The Story of William Clayton*). He was named BYU's distinguished faculty lecturer in 1984 and named a fellow of the Utah State Historical Society in 1988.

Among Allen's most well-known books are *The Story of the Latter-day Saints* (with Glen M. Leonard, Deseret Book Company 2nd edition, 1992) and *Men with a Mission: The Quorum of the Twelve Apostles in the British Isles, 1837–1941* (with Ronald K. Esplin and David J. Whittaker, Deseret Book Company, 1992). He was also the major author-compiler of *Studies in Mormon History, 1830–1997: An Indexed Bibliography* (with Ronald W. Walker and David J. Whittaker, University of Illinois Press, 2000). This remarkable bibliography was heralded by the Mormon History Association and by historians as the most valuable tool yet to appear for students of Latter-day Saint history. J. Michael Hunter of the BYU library continues to update the bibliography database, which is now online at mormonhistory.byu.edu. Allen is married to the former Renée Jones, and they live in Provo, Utah.

See page 177 for detailed biography.

Thomas G. Alexander (1992–2004)

Thomas G. Alexander served as BYU faculty from 1964 to 2004, having also taught at the University of Nebraska at Kearney; Southern Illinois University in Carbondale; the University of California, Berkeley; the University of Utah; and Utah State University. He is an author, co-author, editor, or co-editor of twenty-six books and monographs and 150 articles. He specializes in Utah History, Western History, Environmental History, and Mormon History.

Born in Logan, Utah, on August 8, 1935, Alexander attended the public schools of Ogden, Utah. He earned an associate of science degree from Weber State University in 1955, bachelor's and master's degrees at Utah State University in 1960 and 1961, and a PhD in American history at the University of California, Berkeley, in 1965.

Alexander has been awarded numerous prizes and honors. These include the David and Beatrice Evans Biography Award for *Things in Heaven and Earth*, the Mormon History Association Best Book Award (twice) for *Mormonism in Transition* and *Things in Heaven and Earth*, the Mormon History Association Best Article Award (thrice), the Utah State Historical Society Best Article Award (twice), the Daughters of the American Revolution History Medal Award, the Award of Merit of the American Association for State and Local History, and the Western History Association Award of Merit and Honorary Life Membership. He is a fellow of the Utah State Historical Society and the Utah Academy of Sciences, Arts, and Letters. He has served as president of Phi Alpha Theta; the American Historical Association—Pacific Coast Branch; the Mormon History Association; the Utah Valley Historical Society; and the Utah Academy of Sciences, Arts, and Letters. He is president-elect of the national organization of the Sons of Utah Pioneers. He has served as chair of the Utah Humanities Council, the Utah State Historical Society, and the Provo City Landmarks Commission. He served as parliamentarian of the Western History Association and as a member of the WHA council. He has served on committees for the Organization of American Historians and the American Society for Environmental History.

He and his wife, Marilyn John Alexander, live in Provo. He is active in community and church service. He has served as a neighborhood chairman, as a bishop, in three bishoprics, as a High Priest group leader, and in other positions in the Church. He and his wife served missions in Berlin, Germany, in 2004 and 2005, and in the Family and Church History Mission in Salt Lake City, Utah, in 2005. He currently serves as Sunday School president in his congregation. He and his wife have five grandchildren and six grandchildren.

See chapters 1 and 2, especially page 35, for detailed biography.

Ignacio M. García (2006–present)

Ignacio M. García is a professor of history at BYU and the current holder of the Lemuel Hardison Redd Jr. Endowed Chair in Western American History. García, a pioneer in Mexican American studies, is a prolific historian of the American Southwest. His work illuminates the emergence of Latinos as a major political and cultural force in the region. His scholarly monographs have explored political power in the West, from the ways in which internal dynamics of local organizations interact with the external pressures of racialized power and privilege, to the ways in which reclaimed ethnic and racial identities influence grassroots organizations. A tireless advocate of civil rights and liberties, García cares deeply about those who labor under the weight of prejudice and poverty. He seeks to expand our view of the West by exploring the global connections and implications of this much-studied region.

See page 181 for detailed biography.

JAMES B. ALLEN

James "Jim" B. Allen was born in Ogden, Utah, in 1927. His early years were spent in Star Valley, Wyoming, and in Logan, Utah, where he graduated from high school in 1945. He then served three years in the US Navy and two years as a Latter-day Saint missionary in California. He graduated from Utah State University in 1954, received a master's degree from BYU in 1957, and received a PhD in history from the University of Southern California in 1963.

Allen began his professional career in the Church Education System in 1954. He served as a seminary teacher, a seminary coordinator, an Institute of Religion teacher, and director of the Institutes of Religion in Long Beach and San Bernardino, California. In 1963, he became a member of the religion faculty at BYU, and the following year he joined the history department. In 1972, he was appointed Assistant Church Historian under newly appointed Church Historian Leonard J. Arrington. For the next seven years, he spent half his time in that capacity and the other half at BYU. After returning full time to BYU, he served as chair of the history department from 1981 to 1987, after which he was appointed the Lemuel Hardison Redd Jr. Chair in Western American History. He held this chair until his retirement from BYU in 1992.

To Allen, the term "retire" did not mean "quit." He was soon appointed as a senior research fellow in the Joseph Fielding Smith Institute for LDS History, where he served for a short time on the institute's executive committee. He continued his association with the institute until it was disbanded in 2005. For nearly twenty years after his retirement, he continued to teach an independent study course for BYU.

Throughout his career, Allen has authored, co-authored, or co-edited seventeen books and monographs; around ninety articles, mostly related to Latter-day Saint church history; and numerous book reviews in professional journals. He has received several prizes and awards for his work, including, the prestigious David Woolley Evans and Beatrice Cannon Evans Biography Award in 1986 for *Trials of Discipleship: The Story of William Clayton, A Mormon* (republished in 2002 as *No Toil nor Labor Fear: The Story of William Clayton*). In 1984 he was named Distinguished Faculty Lecturer at BYU. He has also received several "best article" awards given annually by various historical associations, and in 1988, he was named a fellow of the Utah State Historical Society. In 2008, the Mormon History Association gave him the Leonard J. Arrington Award for a Distinctive Contribution to the cause of Mormon History.

Among Allen's most well-known publications, in addition to *Trials of Discipleship*, are *The Story of the Latter-day Saints* (with Glen M. Leonard, Deseret Book Company 2d ed., 1992) and *Men with a Mission: The Quorum of the Twelve Apostles in the British Isles, 1837–1941* (with Ronald K. Esplin and David J. Whittaker, Deseret Book Company, 1992).

Left: Jim and Renée Allen wedding; Right: James B. Allen

He was also the major author-compiler of *Studies in Mormon History, 1830–1997: An Indexed Bibliography* (with Ronald W. Walker and David J. Whittaker, University of Illinois Press, 2000). This remarkable bibliography, which took Allen over sixteen years to compile, was heralded by the Mormon History Association and historians in general as the most valuable tool yet for students of Latter-day Saint history. In 2001 he received a special citation from the Mormon History Association for his work on the project. Working with J. Michael Hunter of the BYU library, Allen continued to update the bibliography database, though eventually Gerrit van Dyk took over that responsibility. The database is now online at mormonhistory.byu.edu and smh.lib.byu.edu.

Allen is also a co-author, with Walker and Whittaker, of *Mormon History* (University of Illinois Press, 2001), a study of the history of historical writing about the Church. His latest book is *Still the Right Place: Utah's Second Half-Century of Statehood, 1945–1995* (Provo and Salt Lake City: Charles Redd Center for Western Studies and the Utah State Historical Society, 2016). In addition, he has reviewed several volumes of the highly important *Joseph Smith Papers* for *BYU Studies Quarterly*.

Allen is married to the former Renée Jones, and they live in Provo, Utah. They are the parents of five (one deceased), grandparents of twenty-one (two deceased), and great-grandparents of twenty-three. From 1999 to 2000, the Allens served a full-time mission at the Boston Institute of Religion. From January to April 2002, they lived in Laie, Hawaii, where Allen taught on a volunteer basis in the history department at BYU–Hawaii. They have both been highly active in The Church of Jesus Christ of Latter-day Saints, serving in many capacities, including leadership positions. From January 2004 until January 2013, they served as officiators in the Mt. Timpanogos Temple. Now, much of Allen's available time is taken up with working on his personal and family history.

Selected Bibliography

Allen is the author, co-author, or co-editor of thirteen books and nearly one hundred articles.

Allen, James B. *The Company Town in the American West*. Norman: University of Oklahoma Press, 1966.

Allen, James B., and Richard O. Cowan. *Mormonism in the Twentieth*

Century. Provo: Brigham Young University Press, 1964; revised edition, 1967.

Allen, James B., and Marvin S. Hill, eds. *Mormonism and American Culture*. New York: Harper & Row, 1972.

Allen, James B., and Thomas G. Alexander, eds. *Manchester Mormons: The Journal of William Clayton, 1840–1842*. Salt Lake City: Peregrine Smith, Inc., 1974.

Allen, James B., and Glen M. Leonard. *The Story of the Latter-day Saints*. Salt Lake City: Deseret Book Company, 1976; 2nd ed. updated and revised, 1992.

Allen, James B., and Thomas G. Alexander. *Mormons and Gentiles: A History of Salt Lake City*. Boulder, CO: Pruett Press, 1984.

Allen, James B., *Trials of Discipleship: The Story of William Clayton, A Mormon*. Urbana: University of Illinois Press, 1987. Revised and republished: *No Toil Nor Labor Fear: The Story of William Clayton*. Provo, UT: Brigham Young University Press, 2002.

Allen, James B., Ronald K. Esplin, and David J. Whittaker. *Men with a Mission: The Quorum of the Twelve Apostles in the British Isles 1837–1840*. Salt Lake City: Deseret Book, 1992.

Allen, J. Michael, and James B. Allen. *World History from 1500*. New York: HarperCollins, 1993.

Allen, James B., Jessie Embry, and Kahlile Mehr. *Hearts Turned to the Fathers: A History of the Genealogical Society of The Church of Jesus Christ of Latter-day Saints*. Provo, UT: BYU Studies Monograph Series, 1995.

Allen, James B., Ronald W. Walker, and David J. Whittaker. *Studies in Mormon History, 1830–1997: An Indexed Bibliography*. Urbana: University of Illinois Press, 2000.

Allen, James B., Ronald W. Walker, and David J. Whittaker. *Mormon History*. Urbana: University of Illinois Press, 2001.

Allen, James B. *Still the Right Place: Utah's Second Half-Century of Statehood, 1945–1995*. Provo and Salt Lake City: Charles Redd Center for Western Studies and Utah State Historical Society, 2016.

IGNACIO M. GARCÍA

Ignacio M. García is the Redd Center's current Lemuel Hardison Redd Jr. Professor of Western and Latino History and has been a faculty member of the Department of History at BYU since 1995. A nationally recognized and respected scholar, he is the author of seven books focusing on Mexican American studies, Latino/a/x history, politics, civil rights, and sports. Two of those books have received commendations. He is also the author of numerous articles, essays, book chapters, and most recently, works on Latino Latter-day Saints, domestically and internationally. He has received numerous awards and recognitions, with the two

Ignacio M. Garcia

most recent being the 2019 James V. Mink Oral History Award and the 2020 Hickman Diversity Lecture Award. Currently, he is working on a book about Eduardo Balderas, the first translator for The Church of Jesus Christ of Latter-day Saints, founder of the *Liahona* magazine, and one of the first Spanish-speaking patriarchs in the Church.

García served as president of the Mormon History Association from 2019 to 2020 and currently serves on the boards of *BYU Studies*, the Global Mormon Studies Association, and several other international journals. He is a founding member of the College of Family, Home, and Social Sciences' Diversity, Collaboration, and Inclusion Committee and currently serves as the committee's chair.

Born in Nuevo Laredo, Mexico, and raised on the west side of San Antonio, Texas, García showed an early passion for writing history that could change the life of his community and the nation. As a young activist for civil rights, he helped organize clubs, labor associations, political entities, and even community newspapers.

He served in Vietnam from 1971 to 1972, where he ran an army dispensary in the Mekong Delta and participated in several mercy missions to villages not serviced by any medical facility. In an interview with the *Church News*, he said, "The war in Vietnam taught me much about my abilities to be compassionate, understanding of others and to make tough and unpopular decisions."

García received a BA in Journalism and Theater from Texas A&I University in 1976, then worked for several years as a journalist covering current events and heading the religion beat. He also had a short stint as a correspondent for the *Tucson Citizen*, covering the civil war in El Salvador. Later, as an independent reporter, he travelled to Lebanon to write about the Palestinian Liberation Organization (PLO). He went back to school and received his MA and PhD in history from the University of Arizona. Two of his books are optioned for feature films.

Selected Publications

García, Ignacio M. *Chicano While Mormon: Activism, War and Keeping the Faith.* Vancouver, BC: Fairleigh Dickinson University Press, 2015.

García, Ignacio M. *When Mexicans Could Play Ball, Basketball, Race, and Identity in San Antonio, 1928–1945.* Austin: University of Texas Press, 2014.

García, Ignacio M. *White but Not Equal: Mexican Americans, Jury Discrimination and the Supreme Court.* Tucson: University of Arizona Press, 2009.

García, Ignacio M. *Hector P. García: In Relentless Pursuit of Justice.* Houston: Arté Público Press, Hispanic Civil Rights Series, 2003.

García, Ignacio M. *Viva Kennedy: Mexican Americans in Search of Camelot*. College Station: Texas A&M University Press, 2000.

García, Ignacio M. *Chicanismo: The Forging of a Militant Ethos among Mexican Americans*. Tucson: University of Arizona Press, 1997).

García, Ignacio M. *United We Win: The Rise and fall of La Raza Unida Party*. Tucson: Mexican American Studies & Research Center (MASRC), University of Arizona, 1989).

APPENDIX 4. MOLLIE AND KARL BUTLER YOUNG SCHOLAR AWARD IN WESTERN STUDIES

The Mollie and Karl Butler Young Scholar Award in Western Studies, sponsored by the Charles Redd Center for Western Studies, was created to promote significant scholarship in western American studies by junior faculty members. The award acknowledges outstanding academic promise, based upon a faculty member's record of research, teaching, and citizenship. The Butler award is funded from the John Topham and Susan Redd Butler Research Endowment, which was established in 1986 through Karl and Mollie Butler.

2021–24	David-James Gonzales, History
2020–23	Mike Taylor, English
2019–22	Scott Sanders, Sociology
2018–21	Adam Brown, Political Science
2017–20	Michelle Kesler, Music
2016–19	James Swensen, Comparative Arts and Letters
2015–18	Mike Searcy, Anthropology
2014–17	Spencer Fluhman, History
2013–16	Sam St. Clair, Plant and Wildlife Sciences
2012–15	Quin Monson, Political Science
2011–14	Brad Barber, Theater and Media Arts

2010–13	None
2009–12	Rick Gill, Biology
2008–11	Jerry Johnson, Biology
2007–10	Sam Otterstrom, Geography
2006–09	Jay H. Buckley, History
2005–08	Jeff Durrant, Geography
2004–07	Dennis Cutchins, English
2003–06	Susan Rugh, History

APPENDIX 5. CLARENCE DIXON TAYLOR RESEARCH AWARDS

Since 1865, the Taylor and Dixon families have contributed to the economic development of Provo and Central Utah. The Clarence Dixon Taylor Award recognizes outstanding scholarship on Central Utah (Utah, Carbon, and Wasatch Counties). Nominations may include theses, books, papers, monographs, articles, symposiums, dramatic presentations, lectures, etc. from students and faculty of Brigham Young University, other institutions, or independent scholars.

2020

Tanner, William W., publisher. "The Settlement of Utah County: Part I," *Pioneer* 67, no. 2 (2020); "The Settlement of Utah County: Part II," *Pioneer* 67, no. 3 (2020).

Hinton, Wayne K. "The Nineteenth-Century Settlement of Utah County." *Pioneer* 67, no. 2 (2020): 2–13.

Carter, D. Robert. "Provo: The Fort Utah Years." *Pioneer* 67, no. 2 (2020): 14–25.

Hunter, J. Michael. "The Early Development of Lehi City." *Pioneer* 67, no. 2 (2020): 26–33.

Wimmer, Sheldon. "Mountainville to Alpine: 1847–1915." *Pioneer* 67, no. 2 (2020): 34–41.

Jessop, Miranda, and Brian Q. Cannon. "Pioneering in Pleasant Grove." *Pioneer* 67, no. 2 (2020): 42–51.

Lawrence, Keith. "The Early Settlement of American Fork." *Pioneer* 67, no. 2 (2020): 52–58.

Orton, Chad. "American Fork: A Leader in Utah's Free Public Education." *Pioneer* 67, no. 2 (2020): 59–64.

Christensen, Allen C. "Historic Alpine Stake Tabernacle." *Pioneer* 67, no. 2 (2020): 65–68

Flick, Roger. "Nineteenth-Century Provo, 1852–1900." *Pioneer* 67, no. 3 (2020): 2–13.

Folkman, Kevin H. "Springville, Utah." *Pioneer* 67, no. 3 (2020): 14–25.

Banks, Bryce S. "Spanish Fork." *Pioneer* 67, no. 3 (2020): 26–33.

Stevenson, L. Dee. "Peteetneet Town: A History of Payson, Utah." *Pioneer* 67, no. 3 (2020): 26–33.

Buckley, Jay H. "Orem: Pioneering on the Provo Bench." *Pioneer* 67, no. 3 (2020): 44–56.

Lawrence, Keith. "Utah County's Other Pioneer Treasures." *Pioneer* 67, no. 3 (2020): 57–67.

2019

Watt, Ronald G. *My Life in Carbon County in the 1950s: A Personal Tour Through Time and Space.* Provo: Scriver Books, 2018.

Winters, Charlene. *City of Orem: A Centennial Benchmark.* San Antonio, TX: Historical Publishing Network, 2019. Photographic history of Orem's centennial.

Lee, Ryan K., and Jay H. Buckley, co-curators; Eric Howard and Carlie Brooks, exhibit designers. Harold B. Lee Library Exhibit. *"Since the Golden Spike: 150 Years of Utah Railroad History."* (2018–19). Exhibit focused upon railroads and their impact on Utah and Wasatch counties.

2018

Carter, D. Robert, *Conflict and Change: Provo, Utah 1857–1859.* Provo: Provo City Corporation, 2017.

Jones, Sondra, *Utah Valley University: 75 Years Strong.* Brookfield, MO: Donning Company Publishers, 2016.

Reiter, Tonya, "Redd Slave Histories: Family, Race, and Sex in Pioneer Utah." *Utah Historical Quarterly* 85 no. 2 (Spring 2017): 109–26.

2017

Walker, Ronald W. "The Tintic War of 1856: A Study of Several Conflicts." *Journal of Mormon History* 42, no. 3 (July 2016): 35–68.

2016

Spangler, Jerry D., and Donna K. *Nine Mile Canyon: The Archaeological History of an American Treasure.* Salt Lake City: University of Utah Press, 2013; and *Last Chance Byway: The History of Nine Mile Canyon.* Salt Lake City: University of Utah Press, 2016.

Whittaker, David. "Joseph B. Keller, Print Culture, and the Modernization of Mormonism, 1885–1918." *BYU Studies* 54, no. 2 (2015): 97–122.

Hunter, Mike, and Jay H. Buckley. "Life in Happy Valley: A Historic Survey of Utah County." L. Tom Perry Special Collections at Brigham Young University's Harold B. Lee Library Gallery Exhibit.

2015

Fillerup, Lisa. "Wasatch Stake Tabernacle—Redefining Pioneers." *Utah Historical Quarterly* 78, no. 3 (2010): 85–108.

2014

Carter, D. Robert. *From Fort to Village: Provo, Utah, 1850–1854.* Provo: Provo City Corporation, 2008.

2010–13

Farmer, Jared. *On Zion's Mount: Mormons, Indians, and the American Landscape.* Cambridge: Harvard University Press, 2010.

Buckley, Jay H., Chase Arnold, Orem Public Library. *Orem [Utah].* Charleston: Arcadia Publishing, 2010.

Handley, George. *Home Waters: A Year of Recompenses on the Provo River.* Salt Lake City: University of Utah Press, 2010.

APPENDIX 6. VISITING FELLOW PROGRAM

The BYU Charles Redd Center for Western Studies invites applications for its Visiting Fellow Program in Western Studies each academic year. University faculty of all ranks, independent scholars, freelance authors, and other public intellectuals who are working on a significant article- or book-length study are eligible to apply for this position. The visiting fellow may be in residence for two to four months during either the fall semester (September–December) or the winter semester (January–April). The center provides a stipend of $2,500 per month of residency, office space, a networked computer, campus library and activity privileges, and limited photocopying and printing. Upon request, the center will also provide a part-time research assistant.

Visiting fellows enjoy library privileges, including access to BYU's extensive western and Mormon archival collections. Major western collections at BYU include the papers of Zane Grey, Gertrude Bonnin (Zitkala Sa), Elizabeth Custer, William Henry Jackson, Charles R. Savage, Thomas F. O'Dea, Arthur Watkins, Reed Smoot, Wallace Bennett, Walter Mason Camp, Earl A. Briningstool, Robert Spurrier Ellison, Finis Ewing, and the Utah Parks Company, as well as over fifty overland trail journals. Major Latter-day Saint collections include the papers of Newell K. Whitney, Hyrum Smith, Emmeline Wells, Thomas and Elizabeth Kane, John Steele, L. John Nuttall, J. Reuben Clark, Adam S. Bennion, David M. Kennedy, Gustive O. Larson, and Ernest L. Wilkinson, as well as a rich array of Latter-day Saint missionary diaries.

Redd Center Fellows

2021	Sheila Nadimi, Visual Arts, John Abbott College, Canada
2021	Luca Criscione, History, Politics, and English, University of Basel, Switzerland
2020	Paul Formisano, English, University of South Dakota
2019	Michael Boyden, American Literature, Uppsala University, Sweden
2018	Vanja Polić, English, University of Zagreb, Croatia
2018	Christopher C. Smith, Postdoctoral Fellow, Utah State University
2017	Tracy L. Brown, Sociology, Anthropology and Social Work, Central Michigan University
2016	William R. Handley, English, University of Southern California
2016	Mariana Whitmer, Center for American Music, University of Pittsburg, Pennsylvania
2016	Jimmy L. Bryan Jr., History, Lamar University, Texas
2014	Jeffrey C. Sanders, History, Washington State University
2014	Randi Lynn Tanglen, English, Austin College, Texas
2014	Kathleen Washburn, English Language and Literature, University of New Mexico
2014	Julianne Newmark, English, New Mexico Tech
2013	Elise Boxer, History, Eastern Washington University
2012–2013	Grisell Ortega Jiménez, Critical Studies, Colegio de Mexico
2012	Christian Heimburger, Modern American History, University of Colorado
2011–2012	Kari Bjarnason, Vestmannaeyjar Library and Archives, Iceland
2011	John G. Turner, History, University of South Alabama

APPENDIX 7. ORAL HISTORY PROJECTS

Harold B. Lee Library, L. Tom Perry Special Collections. Collection: MSS 7752.
Archives.lib.byu.edu/respositories/14/resources/486
Finding aid (2008): John M. Murphy, GlendaLynn Ainsworth, Zann Casper, and Elizabeth Ballif
Donated: Charles Redd Center for Western Studies; recurring donations since 1959.

The library collection contains oral history project case files, audio interviews, and bound transcripts of oral history interviews completed by the Redd Center between 1959 and 2013. In general, case files may contain an analog recording of the interview made by the interviewer, a typed transcript, a corrected transcript, and documents regarding permission to make the documents public signed by the person interviewed. Some case files do not have an accompanying transcription and vice versa.

1. LDS Polygamy Oral History Project transcripts and case files, 1959–1985.
2. Brigham Young University Oral History Project transcripts and case files, 1965–1982.
3. Southeastern Utah Oral History Project transcripts and case files, 1972–1979.
4. Posey War Oral History Project transcripts and case files, 1972–1976.
5. LDS Chaplains Oral History Project transcripts and case files, 1973–

1974.

6. Interstate Brick Company Oral History Project transcripts and case files, 1973–1974.

7. Simpson Springs Oral History Project transcripts and case files, 1973–1976.

8. Labor Oral History Project transcripts and case files, 1973–1979.

9. Charles Redd Oral History Project transcripts and case files, 1973–1979.

10. American Fork Oral History Project transcripts and case files, 1973–1979.

11. Provo City Oral History Project transcripts and case files, 1974–1975.

12. Castle Gate Oral History Project transcripts and case files, 1974–1976.

13. Bamberger Railroad Oral History Project transcripts and case files, 1976.

14. San Rafael Swell Oral History Project transcripts and case files, 1977–1981.

15. Utah Political Oral History Project transcripts and case files, 1979–1980.

16. LDS Family Life Oral History Project transcripts and case files, 1980–1985.

17. African American Oral History Project transcripts, case files, and other material, 1980–1995.

18. Tenth Ward Oral History Project case files, 1987.

19. German–Speaking Immigrants Oral History Project transcripts and case files, 1987–1990.

20. LDS Native American Oral History Project transcripts and case files, 1989–1991, 2007–2008.

21. Geneva Steel Archives Oral History Project transcripts and case files, 1990–1991.

22. LDS Hispanic American Oral History Project transcripts and case files, 1991–2006.

23. World War II Homefront Oral History Project transcripts and case files, 1991–1992.

24. Mexican American Military Oral History Project transcripts and case files, 1991–1995.
25. LDS Polynesian American Oral History Project transcripts and case files, 1991–2004.
26. LDS Missionary Oral History Project transcripts and case files, 1992–1993.
27. US Forest Service Oral History Project transcripts and case files, 1992–1994.
28. Western Aviation Oral History Project transcripts and case files, 1992–1993.
29. Wasatch County Oral History Project transcripts and case files, 1993–1994.
30. Big Horn Basin Oral History Project case file, 1994.
31. LDS Asian American Oral History Project transcripts and case files, 1991–2008.
32. Bonneville Salt Flats Oral History Project transcripts and case files, 1994– 2003.
33. Franklin Neighborhood Oral History Project transcripts and case files, 1997–1999.
34. North Logan, Utah, Oral History Project transcripts and case files, 1998–1999.
35. Utah Universities in Iran Oral History Project transcripts and case files, 1998–1999.
36. Cache Valley Baseball Oral History Project transcripts and case files, 2000.
37. Daughters of Utah Pioneers Oral History Project transcripts and case files, 2001.
38. Utah County Baseball Oral History Project transcripts and case files, 2001–2002.
39. International Women's Year Oral History Project transcripts and case files, 2003–2004.
40. LDS Sports and Recreation Oral History Project transcripts and case files, 2003–2006.
41. Midwives Oral History Project transcripts and case files, 2005.
42. Nurses Training Oral History Project transcripts and case files,

2005–2006.

43. Livestock Oral History Project transcripts and case files, 2005–2006.

44. Redd Center Oral History Project transcripts and case files, 2006–2010.

45. Provo South Stake Oral History Project transcripts and case files, 2008–2009.

46. Santa Fe Oral History Project transcripts and case files, 2008–2009.

47. Family Home Evening Oral History Project transcripts and case files, 2009.

48. San Juan County Public Lands Oral History Project transcripts and case files, 2011.

49. Charles Redd Center for Western History Lectures, approximately 1970–1990.

50. Moore Idaho Lost River Stake Oral History Project transcripts, 1976–1978.

51. American Airpower Heritage Group Oral History Project transcripts, 1992 January 2.

52. Historic Downtown Provo Oral History Project, 1992–2013.

53. Silicon Slopes Oral History Project, 2013–2014.

APPENDIX 8. REDD CENTER PUBLICATIONS

The Redd Center published a monograph series for approximately twenty years. These monographs provided an outlet for publications that were longer than an article but shorter than a book. They also included publication of the Redd Center's monthly lecture series. Around the year 2000 the center decided to offer a subvention for presses to help reduce the per unit costs of books or to provide special features such as color prints. The Redd Center has published books by Jessie L. Embry, Associate Director, based on the Redd Center's oral history projects. These include books on Hispanic-American and Asian-American Latter-day Saints. Embry's book, *Spiritualized Recreation: All-Church Athletic Tournaments and Dance Festivals*, was published as an ebook on the Redd Center site, and this book (as well as many others) can be found at reddcenter.byu.edu/Pages/past-publications. Most recently, the center has hosted summer seminars and then published the best essays in anthologies with academic presses.

The Redd Center also offers Publication Grants for up to $3,000 to assist in the publication of important contributions to studies about the Intermountain West.

Redd Center Monographs, Anthologies, and Publications

Gressley, Gene M. *West by East: The American West in the Gilded Age*. Provo, UT: Brigham Young University Press, 1972.

Townley, John M. *Conquered Provinces: Nevada Moves Southeast, 1864-1871*. Provo, UT: Brigham Young University Press, 1973.

Arrington, Leonard J., Thomas G. Alexander, and Dean May. *A Depen-*

dent Commonwealth: Utah's Economy from Statehood to the Great Depression. Provo, UT: Brigham Young University Press, 1974.

Alexander, Thomas G., ed. Essays on the American West, 1972-1973. Provo, UT: Brigham Young University Press, 1974.

Alexander, Thomas G., ed. Essays on the American West, 1973–74. Provo, UT: Brigham Young University Press, 1975.

Alexander, Thomas G., ed. Essays on the American West, 1974–75. Provo, UT: Brigham Young University Press, 1976.

Hinckley, Robert H., and JoAnn Jacobsen Wells. "I'd Rather be Born Lucky Than Rich": The Autobiography of Robert H. Hinckley. Provo, UT: Brigham Young University Press, 1977.

Alexander, Thomas G., ed. "Soul Butter and Hog Wash" and Other Essays on the American West. Provo, UT: Brigham Young University Press, 1978.

Jackson, Richard H., ed. The Mormon Role in the Settlement of the West. Provo, UT: Brigham Young University Press, 1979.

Alexander, Thomas G., ed. The Mormon People: Their Character and Traditions. Provo, UT: Brigham Young University Press, 1980.

Melville, Keith J. Governor J. Bracken Lee and Margaret Draper Lee. Provo, UT: Charles Redd Center for Western Studies, 1980.

Embry, Jessie L. Richardson Family History: An Oral History Study. Provo, UT: Charles Redd Center for Western Studies, 1982.

Palmer, Richard F., and Karl D. Butler. Brigham Young: The New York Years. Provo, UT: Charles Redd Center for Western Studies, 1982.

Alexander, Thomas G., and John F. Bluth, eds. The Twentieth Century American West: Contributions to an Understanding. Salt Lake City: Signature Books/Charles Redd Center for Western Studies, 1983.

Alexander, Thomas G., and Jessie L. Embry, eds. After 150 Years: The Latter-day Saints in Sesquicentennial Perspective. Provo, UT: Charles Redd Center for Western Studies, 1983.

Embry, Jessie L. La Sal Reflections: A Redd Family Journal. Anaheim, CA: Charles Redd Foundation, 1984.

Embry, Jessie L., and Howard A. Christy, eds. Community Development in the American West: Past and Present Nineteenth and Twentieth Century Frontiers. Salt Lake City: Signature Books/Charles Redd

Center for Western Studies, 1985.

McCarthy, Max R. *The Last Chance Canal Company.* Salt Lake City: Signature Books/Charles Redd Center for Western Studies, 1987.

Layton, Stanford J. *To No Privileged Class.* Salt Lake City: Signature Books/Charles Redd Center for Western Studies, 1988.

Gomez, Arthur R. *A Most Singular Country: A History of Occupation in the Big Bend.* Salt Lake City: Signature Books/Charles Redd Center for Western Studies, 1990.

Work, James C. *Following Where the River Begins: A Personal Essay on an Encounter with the Colorado River.* Salt Lake City: Signature Books/Charles Redd Center for Western Studies, 1991.

Palmer, Richard F., and Karl D. Butler. *Brigham Young: The New York Years.* Salt Lake City: Signature Books/Charles Redd Center for Western Studies, rev. ed.,1992.

McPherson, Robert S. *Sacred Land, Sacred View.* Boulder: University Press of Colorado, 1992.

Bartholomew, Rebecca, and Leonard J. Arrington. *Rescue of the 1856 Handcart Company.* Salt Lake City: Signature Books/Charles Redd Center for Western Studies, reprint, 1993.

Arrington, Leonard J. *Charles Redd: Utah's Audacious Stockman.* Logan: Utah State University Press/Charles Redd Center for Western Studies, 1995.

Harris, John S. *Second Crop: Poems by John Sterling Harris.* Provo, UT: Charles Redd Center for Western Studies, 1996.

Howe, Susan. *Stone Spirits: Poems by Susan Elizabeth Howe.* Provo, UT: Charles Redd Center for Western Studies, 1997.

Embry, Jessie L. *"In His Own Language": Mormon Spanish Speaking Congregations in the United States.* Provo, UT: Charles Redd Center for Western Studies, 1997.

Embry, Jessie L. *Asian American Mormons: Bridging Culture.* Provo, UT: Charles Redd Center for Western Studies, 1999.

Embry, Jessie L. *North Logan Oral History Project: Lyle and Nancy Crookston Israelsen.* Provo, UT: Charles Redd Center for Western Studies, 2000.

Embry, Jessie L. *Spiritualized Recreation: Mormon All-Church Athletic*

Tournaments and Dance Festivals. Provo, UT: Charles Redd Center for Western Studies, 2008, ebook.

Embry, Jessie L. *"En Su Propia Lengua": Congregaciones Mormonas de Hispanoparlantes En Los Estados Unidos.* Provo, UT: Charles Redd Center for Western Studies, 2009.

Cannon, Brian Q., and Jessie L. Embry, eds. *Utah in the Twentieth Century.* Logan, UT: Utah State University Press, 2009.

Walker, Ronald W. *Wayward Saints: The Social and Religious Protests of the Godbeites Against Brigham Young.* Provo, UT: Brigham Young University Press, 2009.

Smith, Charlotte Palfreyman, ed. *San Juan Public Lands.* Provo, UT: Charles Redd Center for Western Studies, 2011.

Smith, Charlotte Palfreyman, ed. *Stories Told: Life on the Public Lands in San Juan County.* Provo, UT: Charles Redd Center for Western Studies, 2012.

Embry, Jessie L., ed. *Oral History, Community, and Work in the American West.* Tucson: University of Arizona Press, 2013.

Embry, Jessie L., and Brian Q. Cannon, eds. *Immigrants in the Far West: Historical Identities and Experiences.* Salt Lake City: University of Utah Press, 2015.

Hartley, William G. *Faithful and Fearless: Major Howard Egan, Early Mormonism and the Pioneering of the American West.* Provo, UT: Charles Redd Center for Western Studies, 2017.

Allen, James B. *Still the Right Place: Utah's Second Half-Century of Statehood, 1945–1995.* Provo, UT: Charles Redd Center for Western Studies, 2017.

Milner, Clyde A. II, and Brian Q. Cannon, eds. *Reconstruction and Mormon America.* Norman: University of Oklahoma Press, 2019.

Rogers, Jedediah S., and Matthew C. Godfrey, eds. *The Earth Will Appear as the Garden of Eden: Essays on Mormon Environmental History.* Salt Lake City: University of Utah Press, 2019.

Hafen, P. Jane, and Brenden W. Rensink, eds. *Essays on American Indian and Mormon History.* Salt Lake City: University of Utah Press, 2019.

Rensink, Brenden W., ed. *The North American West in the 21st Century.* Lincoln: University of Nebraska Press, 2022.

Redd Center Publication Grant Recipients

The Redd Center offers publication grants ranging from $1,000 to $3,000 to presses to help offset the costs of publishing Intermountain West titles. Grants permit presses to improve the quality of the publication and/or make the book more affordable.

Janetski, Joel C. *Clear Creek Canyon Archaeological Project (Five Finger Ridge): Results and Synthesis.* Provo, UT: Brigham Young University Press, 2000.

Dufurrena, Linda, and Carolyn Dufurrena. *Fifty Miles from Home: Riding the Long Circle on a Nevada Family Ranch.* Reno: University of Nevada Press, 2002.

Baumler, Ellen, and Margaret Ronan. *Girl from the Gulches: The Story of Mary Ronan.* Helena: Montana Historical Society Press, 2003.

Hadley, C.J. *Trappings of the Great Basin Buckaroo.* Reno: University of Nevada Press, 2003.

Hatch, Charles, and Todd Compton, eds. *A Widows Tale: The 1884-1896 Diary of Helen Mar Kimball Whitney.* Logan: Utah State University Press, 2003.

Hausladen, Gary. *Western Places, American Myths: How We Think about the West.* Reno: University of Nevada Press, 2003.

McPherson, Robert S. *Navajo Land, Navajo Culture: The Utah Experience in the Twentieth Century.* Norman: University of Oklahoma Press, 2003.

Rathbun, Daniel C. B., and David V. Alexander. *New Mexico Frontier Military Place Names.* Las Cruces, NM: Yucca Tree Press, 2003.

Topping, Gary. *Utah Historians and the Reconstruction of Western History.* Norman: University of Oklahoma Press, 2003.

Goin, Peter, and C. Elizabeth Raymond. *Changing Mines in America.* Santa Fe: Center for American Places, 2004.

Goin, Peter, and Paul F. Starrs, *Black Rock.* Reno: University of Nevada Press, 2005.

Knack, Martha C. *Boundaries Between: The Southern Paiutes, 1775-1995.* Lincoln: University of Nebraska Press, 2005.

Northwest Band of the Shoshone Nation. *Coyote Steals Fire: A Shosho-*

ne Tale. Logan: Utah State University Press, 2005.

Logan, Michael F. *The Lessening Stream: An Environmental History of the Santa Cruz River.* Tucson: University of Arizona Press, 2006.

Paulson, Deborah, and William Lawrence Baker. *The Nature of Southwestern Colorado: Recognizing Human Legacies and Restoring Natural Places.* Boulder: University Press of Colorado, 2006

Sheridan, Thomas E. *Landscapes of Fraud: Mission Tumacácori, the Baca Float, and the Betrayal of the O'odham.* Tucson: University of Arizona Press, 2006.

Stacey, Peter B., et. al. *A User's Guide for the Rapid Assessment of the Functional Condition of Stream-Riparian Ecosystems in the American Southwest.* Salt Lake City: Wild Utah Project, 2006.

Swibold, Dennis L. *Copper Chorus: Mining, Politics, and the Montana Press, 1889-1959.* Helena: Montana State Historical Society, 2006.

Whitley, Colleen. *From the Ground Up: A History of Mining in Utah.* Logan: Utah State University, 2006.

Colwell-Chanthaphonh, Chip. *Massacre at Camp Grant: Forgetting and Remembering Apache History.* Tucson: University of Arizona Press, 2007.

Bsumek, Erika. *Indian-Made: Navajo Culture in the Marketplace, 1880-1940.* Lawrence: University Press of Kansas, 2008.

Horton, D. Seth. *New Stories of the Southwest.* Athens: Swallow Press/ Ohio University Press, 2008.

Smart, William B. *Mormonism's Last Colonizer: The Life and Times of William H. Smart.* Logan: Utah State University Press, 2008.

Cannon, Brian Q., and Jessie L. Embry, eds. *Utah in the Twentieth Century.* Logan: Utah State University Press, 2009.

Grow, Matthew. *"Liberty to the Downtrodden": Thomas L. Kane, Romantic Reformer.* New Haven: Yale University Press, 2009.

Larkin, Karin, and Randall H. McGuire. *The Archaeology of Class War: The Colorado Coalfield Strike of 1913-1914.* Boulder: University Press of Colorado, 2009.

McPherson, Robert S. *Comb Ridge and Its People: The Ethnohistory of a Rock.* Logan: Utah State University Press, 2009.

Tatum, Stephen. *In the Remington Moment.* Lincoln: University of Nebraska Press, 2010.

Mackedon, Michon. *Bombast: Spinning Atoms in the Desert*. Reno: Blackrock Institute Press, 2011.

Lawrence, Adrea. *Lessons from an Indian Day School: Negotiating Colonization in Northern New Mexico, 1902–1907*. Lawrence: University Press of Kansas, 2011.

Amundson, Michael A. *Passage to Wonderland: Rephotographing Joseph Stimson's Views of the Cody Road to Yellowstone National Park, 1903 and 2008*. Boulder: University of Colorado Press, 2012.

Baker, Gretchen. *Great Basin National Park: A Guide to the Park and Surrounding Area*. Logan: Utah State University Press, 2012.

Straight, Nathan. *Autobiography, Ecology, and the Well-Placed Self: The Growth of Natural Biography in Contemporary American Life Writing*. New York: Peter Lang, 2012.

Dillon, Mark C. *The Montana Vigilantes 1863-1870: Gold, Guns, and Gallows*. Logan: Utah State University Press, 2013.

Eliason, Eric A., and Tom Mould. *Latter-day Lore: Mormon Folklore Studies* Salt Lake City: University of Utah Press, 2013.

Alexander, Thomas G. *Edward Hunter Snow: Pioneer, Educator, Statesman*. Norman: Arthur H. Clark, 2014.

Carter, Thomas. *Building Zion: The Material World of Mormon Settlement*. Minneapolis: University of Minnesota Press, 2015.

Childers, Leisl Carr. *The Size of the Risk: Histories of Multiple Use in the Great Basin*. Norman: University of Oklahoma Press, 2015.

Embry, Jesse L., and Brian Q. Cannon, eds. *Immigrants in the Far West: Historical Identities and Experiences*. Salt Lake City: University of Utah Press, 2015.

Hogue, Michel. *Metis and the Medicine Line: Creating a Border and Dividing a People* Regina, SK: University of Regina Press, 2015.

Jones, Karen R. *Epiphany in the Wilderness: Hunting Nature and Performance in the Nineteenth-Century American West*. Boulder: University of Colorado Press/Utah State University Press, 2015.

Thompson, Sally. *People Before the Park: The Kootenai and Blackfeet before Glacier National Park*. Helena: Montana Historical Society, 2015.

Frisbee, Meg. *Counterpunch: The Cultural Battles Over Heavyweight Prizefighting in the American West.* Seattle: University of Washington Press, 2016.

Klein, Benjamin. *Irwin Klein and the New Settlers: Photographs of Counterculture in New Mexico.* Lincoln: University of Nebraska Press, 2016.

Wei, William. *Asians in Colorado: A History of Persecution in the Centennial State.* Seattle: University of Washington Press, 2016.

Prince, Stephen L. *Hosea Stout: Lawman, Legislator, Mormon Defender* Boulder: University Press of Colorado, 2017.

Gulliford, Andrew. *The Woolly West: Colorado's Hidden History of Sheepscapes.* College Station: Texas A&M University Press, 2018.

Sabol, Steven. *"A Touch of Civilization": Comparing American and Russian Internal Colonization.* Boulder: University Press of Colorado, 2018.

Swensen, James. *In a Rugged Land: Ansel Adams, Dorothea Lange, and the Three Mormon Towns Collaboration, 1953-1954.* Salt Lake City: University of Utah Press, 2018.

Milner, Clyde A. II, and Brian Q. Cannon, eds. *The Era of Reconstruction in Mormon America*, Norman: University of Oklahoma Press, 2019.

Schofield, Rebecca. *Outriders: Rodeo at the Fringes of the American West.* Seattle: University of Washington Press, 2019.

Eliason, Eric A., and Carol Edison, eds., *This the Plate: Utah Food Traditions.* Salt Lake City: University of Utah Press, 2020.

Stevens, Mikel R., et. al., *The Heart of Penstemon Country: A Natural History of Penstemons in the Utah Region.* Helena, MT: Sweetgrass Books, 2020.

Harrison, Christian S. *All the Water the Law Allows: Las Vegas and Colorado River Politics.* Norman: University of Oklahoma Press, 2021.

King, Farina Noelani, Michael P. Taylor, and James R. Swensen. *Returning Home: Diné Creative Works from the Intermountain Indian School.* Tucson: University of Arizona Press, 2021.

Johnson, Michael K. *A Black Woman's West: The Life of Rose B. Gordon.* Helena: Montana Historical Society, 2022.

APPENDIX 9: *WRITING WESTWARD* PODCAST

Writing Westward features conversations with writers of the North American West, sampling from a variety of disciplines and subfields. The podcast is hosted and produced by the Redd Center associate director and associate history professor Brenden W. Rensink.

Episode List:

038—James McGrath Morris: *Tony Hillerman: A Life* (Feb. 2022)

037—Ryanne Pilgeram: *Pushed Out: Contested Development and Rural Gentrification in the US West* (Jan. 2022)

036—Andrea Ross: *Unnatural Selection: A Memoir of Adoption and Wilderness* (Aug. 2021)

035—Erika Allen Wolters and Brent S. Steel: *The Environmental Politics & Policy of Western Public Lands* (July 2021)

034—Benjamin Hoy: *A Line of Blood and Dirt: Creating the Canada-United States Border across Indigenous Lands* (June 2021)

033—Steven L. Peck: *The Tragedy of King Lear in a Post-Apocalyptic West* (May 2021)

032—Tiffany Midge: *Bury My Heart at Chuck E. Cheese's* (Apr. 2021)

031—Susan Lee Johnson: *Writing Kit Carson: Fallen Heroes in a Changing West* (Mar. 2021)

030—Janne Lahti: *The American West and the World: Transnational and Comparative Perspectives* (Feb. 2021)

029—James R. Skillen: *This Land is My Land: Rebellion in the West* (Jan. 2021)

028—Bathsheba Demuth: *Floating Coast: An Environmental History of the Bering Strait* (Dec. 2020)

027—Barney Scout Mann: *Journeys North: The Pacific Crest Trail* (Nov. 2020)

026—Sherry L. Smith: *Bohemians West: Free Love, Family, and Radicals in Twentieth Century America* (Oct. 2020)

025—Kenneth F. Dewey, Dan O'Brien, & Larkin Powell: *Great Plains Weather, Bison, & Birds* (Sept. 2020)

024—Justin Farrell: *Billionaire Wilderness: The Ultra-Wealthy and the Remaking of the American West* (Aug. 2020)

023—Jeff Metcalf: *Back Cast: Fly-Fishing and Other Such Matters* (July 2020)

022—Maurice Crandall: *These People Have Always Been a Republic: Indigenous Electorates in the U.S.-Mexico Borderlands, 1598-1912* (June 2020)

021—Robert Lee: *Land-grab Universities* (May 2020)

020—Miroslava Chávez-García: *Migrant Longing: Letter Writing Across the U.S.-Mexico Borderlands* (Apr. 2020)

019—Monica Muñoz Martinez: *The Injustice Never Leaves You: Anti-Mexican Violence in Texas* (Mar. 2020)

018—Megan Kate Nelson: *The Three-Cornered War: The Union, the Confederacy, and Native Peoples in the Fight for the West* (Feb. 2020)

017—Jack Nisbet: *The Dreamer and the Doctor: A Forest Lover and a Physician on the Edge of the Frontier* (Jan. 2020)

016—Frank Bergon: *Two-Buck Chuck & The Marlboro Man: The New Old West* (Dec. 2019)

015—Manu Karuka: *Empire's Tracks: Indigenous Nations, Chinese Workers, and the Transcontinental Railroad* (Nov. 2019)

014—Rebecca Robinson and Stephen Strom: *Voices and Views from Bears Ears* (Oct. 2019)

013—Leah Sottile: *The Bundyville Podcast and Longform Western Journalism* (Sept. 2019)

012—Debra Gwartney: *I Am a Stranger Here Myself* (Aug. 2019)

011—Eric P. Perramond: *Unsettled Waters: Rights, Law, and Identity in the American West* (July 2019)

010—John Branch: *The Last Cowboys: A Pioneer Family in the New*

West (June 2019)

009—David A. Chang: *The World and All Things Upon It: Native Hawaiian Geographies of Exploration* (May 2019)

008—Beth Lew-Williams: *The Chinese Must Go: Violence, Exclusion, and the Making of the Alien in America* (Apr. 2019)

007—Terence Young: *Heading Out: A History of American Camping* (Mar. 2019)

006—Flannery Burke: *A Land Apart: The Southwest and the Nation in the Twentieth Century* (Feb. 2019)

005—Tacey M. Atsitty: *Rain Scald: Poems* (Jan. 2019)

004—Stephen Pyne: *Fire in the American West* (Dec. 2018)

003—Benjamin Johnson: *Escaping the Dark Gray City: Fear and Hope in Progressive-Era Conservation* (Nov. 2018)

002—Victoria Lamont: *Westerns: A Women's History* (Oct. 2018)

001—Louis S. Warren: *God's Red Son: The Ghost Dance Religion and the Making of Modern America* (Sept. 2018)

APPENDIX 10. REDD CENTER ANNUAL AWARDS

Instructions for submitting an application:

To apply for an award, visit the Redd Center website (reddcenter.byu. edu), and click on "Apply for an Award." Complete your application. After you have submitted it, you will receive a confirmation message and email. If applicable, please explain whether ongoing COVID-19 pandemic restrictions on travel and other activities will affect your project, and how, detailing potential plans to work amidst restrictions.

Student Award Categories

Annaley Naegle Redd Student Award in Women's History

The Annaley Naegle Redd Student Award in Women's History will be given each year to one undergraduate or graduate student doing research on women in the American West (west of the Mississippi River). It is named after Annaley Naegle Redd, a prominent southeastern Utah rancher and philanthropist and wife of Charles Redd. Awards may be used for any worthy project including preparation of seminar papers, theses, and dissertations. The award is a $1,500 grant to be used for research support (supplies, travel, etc.). The funds cannot be used for salary or capital equipment. Applicants not receiving the Annaley Naegle Redd Award will be considered for the Redd Center's other student grants ($1,500 maximum) if the study area is in the intermountain regions of Arizona, Colorado, Idaho, Montana, Nevada, New Mexico, Utah, or Wyoming. Proposals in all areas of the humanities, arts, and social sciences are welcomed.

Research Award for BYU Upper Division and Graduate Students

The Charles Redd Center for Western Studies invites applications from BYU upper division and graduate students for awards for research dealing with the intermountain regions of Arizona, Colorado, Idaho, Montana, Nevada, New Mexico, Utah, or Wyoming. Awards may be used for any worthy project including preparation of seminar papers, theses, and dissertations. The funds are to be used for research support (supplies, travel, etc.) and not as a salary or for capital equipment. The amount of money awarded will be determined by the research needs as indicated in the application. The maximum amount for this award is normally $1,500. In exceptional cases, the center will consider applications for more money if the applicant offers a strong justification for a larger award. Research may be conducted at any location.

Research Award for Off-Campus Upper Division and Graduate Students

The Charles Redd Center for Western Studies invites applications from upper division and graduate students from any institution of higher learning for awards for research dealing with the intermountain regions of Arizona, Colorado, Idaho, Montana, Nevada, New Mexico, Utah, or Wyoming. Awards may be used for any worthy project including preparation of seminar papers, theses, and dissertations. The funds are to be used for research support (supplies, travel, etc.) and not as a salary or for capital equipment. The amount of money awarded will be determined by the research needs as indicated in the application. The maximum amount for this award is normally $1,500. In exceptional cases, the center will consider applications for more money if the applicant offers a strong justification for a larger award. Research may be conducted at any location.

Senior Seminar/Capstone Project Grant (*BYU students only*)

Charles Redd Center Senior Seminar/Capstone Project Awards will be given each year to BYU undergraduate students who are writing a paper on some aspect of the American West. The award of up to $500 can be used to cover gasoline, parking, copying, travel, and lodging expenses.

Faculty Award Categories

Annaley Naegle Redd Research Assistantship (*BYU faculty only*)

Annaley Naegle Redd Research Assistantships facilitate research on the American West by BYU faculty in any department. Grants of up to $12,000 enable faculty members to hire upper-division undergraduate or graduate students of their choice to work as research assistants on significant projects dealing with Western American studies. Rates of pay for research assistants should be commensurate with the wage scale for student assistants in the faculty member's department. The term of employment for the research assistant is flexible. Preference will be given to applications that show clear benefits in terms of mentoring and acquisition of skills for students who are hired as research assistants. Assistants may be hired for a term, a semester, or a year.

Charles Redd Fellowship Award in Western American History

Fellowship awards of $1,000–$3,500 will be made on an annual basis to students and scholars interested in pursuing research in the intermountain regions of Arizona, Colorado, Idaho, Montana, Nevada, New Mexico, Utah, or Wyoming at the Harold B. Lee Library L. Tom Perry Special Collections. Each award will fund up to one month's research in Special Collections. Award funds are to be used for research support, including travel and lodging expenses, but not as salary. The amount of the fellowship award will be determined by the research needs of the applicant. Awards are to be used for scholarly projects including preparation of seminar papers, theses, dissertations, monographs, and book length projects. Established in 1956, Special Collections has a large department of full-time curators. Manuscript collections number more than nine thousand, almost one million photographic images are held by the L. Tom Perry Special Collections, and more than three-hundred thousand rare books are available for use, along with extensive manuscript materials documenting 19th- and 20th-century Western American history.

Interdisciplinary Studies Grant

The Charles Redd Center for Western Studies invites applications for interdisciplinary research grants of up to $10,000. Applications will be evaluated based upon the following criteria: Does the topic deal with the Intermountain West? This is defined as portions of Arizona, Colorado, Idaho, Montana, Nevada, New Mexico, Utah, and Wyoming. Does the project include researchers representing at least three separate disciplines? At least two of the researchers must be BYU faculty members. One researcher may be a faculty member at another university. Is each discipline's contribution unique and integral to the project? What will be the outcome of the project? Is the budget reasonable? (The budget can include conference and publication expenses.) What else has been done on the research topic? How is this project unique? What is the feasibility of the research plan? Is the project intellectually rigorous?

John Topham and Susan Redd Butler BYU Faculty Research Award
(*BYU faculty only*)
The Charles Redd Center for Western Studies invites applications for research awards funded by the Research Endowment. The proposed research should increase knowledge and understanding of the intermountain regions of Arizona, Colorado, Idaho, Montana, Nevada, New Mexico, Utah, or Wyoming. Applicants should be faculty members at BYU. Both new and ongoing projects are eligible. Award funds are to be used for research support and not as a salary. The amount of the award will be determined by the research needs as indicated in the application, up to a maximum of $3,000. Research may be conducted at any location.

John Topham and Susan Redd Butler Off-Campus Faculty Research Award
The Charles Redd Center for Western Studies invites applications for research awards funded by the John Topham and Susan Redd Butler Research Endowment. The proposed research should increase knowledge and understanding of the intermountain regions of Arizona, Colorado, Idaho, Montana, Nevada, New Mexico, Utah, or Wyoming. Applicants should be faculty members at an institution of higher learning. Both new and ongoing projects are eligible. Award funds are to be used for research support and not as a salary. The amount of the award will

be determined by the research needs as indicated in the application, up to a maximum of $3,000. Research may be conducted at any location.

Visiting Lecturer Program (*BYU faculty only*)
The Charles Redd Center will provide funds for BYU departments to bring visiting lecturers in western studies to BYU. The center provides a stipend up to $300, reasonable travel costs, food, and lodging. Applications are accepted at any time during the year.

Visiting Fellow Program
The Charles Redd Center for Western Studies at Brigham Young University invites applications for its Visiting Fellow Program in Western Studies each academic year. University faculty of all ranks, independent scholars, freelance authors, and other public intellectuals who are working on a significant article- or book-length study are eligible to apply for this position. The visiting fellow may be in residence for two to four months during either the Fall Semester (September–December) or the Winter Semester (January–April). The center will provide a stipend of $2,500 per month of residency, office space, a networked computer, campus library and activity privileges, and limited photocopying and printing. Upon request, the center will provide a part-time research assistant. Please note that due to current university licensing policy, visiting fellows may need to provide their own personal or university login credentials to use Microsoft Office Suite and other licensed applications.

Visiting Fellows will enjoy library privileges, including access to BYU's extensive western and Mormon archival collections. Major western collections at BYU include the papers of Zane Grey, Gertrude Bonnin (Zitkala Sa), Elizabeth Custer, William Henry Jackson, Charles R. Savage, Thomas F. O'Dea, Arthur Watkins, Reed Smoot, Wallace Bennett, Walter Mason Camp, Earl A. Briningstool, Robert Spurrier Ellison, Finis Ewing, and the Utah Parks Company as well as over fifty overland trail journals. Major Latter-day Saint collections include the papers of Newell K. Whitney, Hyrum Smith, Emmeline Wells, Thomas and Elizabeth Kane, John Steele, L. John Nuttall, J. Reuben Clark, Adam S. Bennion, David M. Kennedy, Gustive O. Larson, and Ernest

L. Wilkinson as well as a rich array of Latter-day Saint missionary diaries.

Mollie and Karl Butler Young Scholar Award (*BYU faculty only*)

The Butler Young Scholar Award in Western Studies was created to promote significant scholarship in Western American studies by junior faculty members. This Redd Center award acknowledges outstanding academic promise, based upon a faculty member's record of research, teaching, and citizenship. John Topham and Susan Redd Butler Research Endowment funds the award. Karl and Mollie Butler were instrumental in establishing this endowment in 1986, and it is named in their honor. The award carries a $3,000 annual salary stipend and a $5,000 annual research support award, subject to all university financial policies, and with any capital equipment purchased from these funds becoming the property of the university. Any unused funding may carry over for the duration of the award. Appointments are for three consecutive years and may not be renewed. Any accumulated funding not expended within three (3) years after the expiration of a Young Scholar Award will revert to the Charles Redd Center for reallocation. A faculty member should have been in a faculty position for at least three years, but not more than ten years since completing the terminal degree, and in a rank of Assistant or Associate Professor. The faculty member should be engaged in significant scholarship in Western American studies and is nominated by his/her department chair. If interested, please contact your department chair and arrange for a complete nomination packet. This packet should include a detailed description of what "western" projects the candidate will pursue in the following three to five years.

General Award Categories

Clarence Dixon Taylor Award

Since 1865, the Taylor and Dixon families have contributed to the economic development of Provo and central Utah. The Clarence Dixon Taylor Award recognizes outstanding scholarship about central Utah (Utah, Carbon, and Wasatch counties). Nominations may include theses, books, papers, monographs, articles, symposiums, dramatic presentations, lectures, etc. from students and faculty of BYU, other institutions, or independent scholars. Significant scholarship will be recognized with a maximum of $5,000 awarded for major achievements.

Clarence Dixon Taylor Research Grant

The Clarence Dixon Taylor Research Grant is named for a representative of the Taylor and Dixon families who established an endowment in memory of these families' contribution to the economic development of Provo and central Utah. The grant provides up to $1,500 to encourage and facilitate research about central Utah (Utah, Carbon, and Wasatch Counties). The funds are to be used for research support, including travel and lodging expenses, and will be determined by the research needs of the applicant. The funds cannot be used for salary or capital equipment. Expected research outcomes include articles, monographs, books, theses, dissertations, symposiums, dramatic presentations, lectures, etc. Undergraduate and graduate students, independent scholars, and academic faculty are all invited to apply. Proposals in all areas of the arts, humanities, and social sciences are welcomed.

Independent Research and Creative Work Award

The Redd Center invites applications from individuals who are not connected to a college or university, and who are interested in researching or writing on some aspect of the intermountain regions of Arizona, Colorado, Idaho, Montana, Nevada, New Mexico, Utah, and Wyoming. Both new and ongoing projects are eligible. Award funds are for research support and not salary. The amount of the award will be determined by the research needs, up to a maximum of $1,500.

Public Programming Award

The Redd Center invites applications from private or public organizations for its public programming award. Any organization planning a conference, museum exhibit, lecture series or similar public program may apply. The proposed program should increase knowledge and understanding of the intermountain regions of Arizona, Colorado, Idaho, Montana, Nevada, New Mexico, Utah, or Wyoming. Advertising for the project should list the Charles Redd Center as a sponsor. The award carries a stipend of up to $3,000. The funds may be used for research or the actual costs of presenting the program and may be used as a cash match for funding from a state, national humanities, arts council. New programs and special aspects of ongoing projects are eligible. Please note that indirect costs are not eligible through this award.

Publication Grant (*presses only*)
The Redd Center gives grants of up to $3,000 to academic publishers to assist in the publication of scholarly studies on Arizona, Colorado, Idaho, Montana, Nevada, New Mexico, Utah, or Wyoming. The grant helps offset publication costs in order to lower the book's selling price. The book should have been accepted for publication and be ready for publication but not yet printed. If funded, acknowledgment to the center must be included inside the publication.

CPSIA information can be obtained
at www.ICGtesting.com
Printed in the USA
JSHW030454220422
24916JS00001B/3